CONTENTS

53 BOATS
You Can Build

53
BOATS
You Can Build

with commentary by
Richard Henderson

International Marine Publishing Company
Camden, Maine

© 1985 by International Marine Publishing Company

Typeset by Journal Publications, Inc., Camden, Maine
Printed and bound by BookCrafters, Inc., Chelsea, Michigan

Published by International Marine Publishing Company
21 Elm Street, Camden, Maine
(207) 236-4342

Library of Congress Cataloging in Publication Data

Henderson, Richard, 1924–
    53 boats you can build.

    Includes index.
    1. Boatbuilding.   I. Title   II. Title: Fifty-three boats you can build.
VM351.H47   1985   623.8'223   84-47853
ISBN 0-87742-185-4

L. FRANCIS HERRESHOFF

AL MASON

C. W. PAINE

MURRAY J. PETERSON

FENWICK C. WILLIAMS

CHARLES W. WITTHOLZ

INTRODUCTION

E.B. White once wrote, "It is small wonder that men hold boats in the secret place of their mind, almost from the cradle to the grave." That secret place of the mind is often a source of fantasy when sailors dream of building their own perfect boat and taking her to idyllic harbors.

This book is a collection of boat designs that can help turn such fantasies into reality, an important reason being that building many of the boats herein is truly within the means of a devoted sailor. The designers of these craft have taken pains to simplify construction for economical building by professionals and, in many cases, ease of construction for backyard amateurs. Large-scale plans and, in some cases, building instructions are available from the designers listed in the back of the book. The majority of plans calls for wood construction — carvel, lapstrake, or plywood — but there are also plans for both one-off fiberglass and steel construction.

The collection has something for almost any sailor (except the all-out racer), whether he wants to poke into secluded gunkholes, sail away to far-off places, or merely attract admiring glances in his home waters. There are pulling boats, sharpies, dories, catboats, canoe yawls, sailing dinghies, cat ketches, live-aboard boats, offshore passagemakers, club racers, and coastal cruisers. About the only sailboats you won't find are IOR-type "grand prix" racers and large, complicated luxury yachts.

The designers whose work is presented here are well-recognized, highly respected naval architects, as well as experienced boatmen. Most have practiced for many decades, and their work has been thoroughly tested and proven. You'll find that their designs, by and large, tend toward the traditional and are sometimes inspired by historic workboat types. Occasionally, some speed is traded for ease of construction or seaworthiness; most of the boats on these pages are supremely practical and functional. Then, too, they are interesting to behold, even beautiful. At the least, they have a certain character that sets them apart from many of the standard stock boats that are mass produced.

These designs are taken from a number of books that have been published by International Marine. The book in which each design previously appeared is given at the end of its commentary.

It has been a privilege introducing this distinguished design collection and commenting on the individual craft. I feel it is important for boating neophytes to recognize there is a healthy alternative to the kind of stock boats that have been strongly influenced by the rating rules and by the boating stylists, many of whom, I suspect, know not the real demands of the sea.

Richard Henderson
Gibson Island, Maryland

53 BOATS
You Can Build

JOHN ATKIN

1

Nina

Length: 11 feet 4 inches
Beam: 4 feet 7 inches
Draft: 4½ inches
Sail Area: 77 square feet
Designer: John Atkin

When you think of father-and-son yacht designers, you might think first of Nat Herreshoff and L. Francis or perhaps Edward Burgess and Starling, but surely no boat buff would overlook William "Billy" Atkin and his son John. Atkin boats are traditional, practical, and nearly always exceptionally pleasing to the eye. John, who is a well-known yacht surveyor as well as a designer, carries on in the tradition of his father, but with an open mind toward the latest materials and methods of construction.

Nina is John Atkin's concept of a practical, rowable centerboard sailing skiff that an amateur builder can build inexpensively. The flat-bottom design affords high initial stability and ease of construction. Although the plans show cross planks on her bottom, I would prefer marine plywood for its smoother surface and lack of seams. The topsides are clinker built, and the curves of the lapped seams, which follow the pronounced sheerline, give the boat a most appealing look.

A roomy boat, *Nina* is capable of carrying two adults or three children under sail and, of course, more when she is propelled by an "ash breeze." She has thwarts and thole pins for two rowing positions. The gaff sail provides plenty of area without the need of a tall mast.

Although *Nina* is not as smart or fast as a modern lightweight "skimming dish," she should move well in a breeze and be a good ghoster in light airs. I would want to add flotation under the thwarts to simplify bailing out after swamping. But even without flotation, she will not sink; and she is not easily capsized, particularly with her reefable sail.

Plans from Practical Small Boat Designs *by John Atkin, International Marine, 1983*

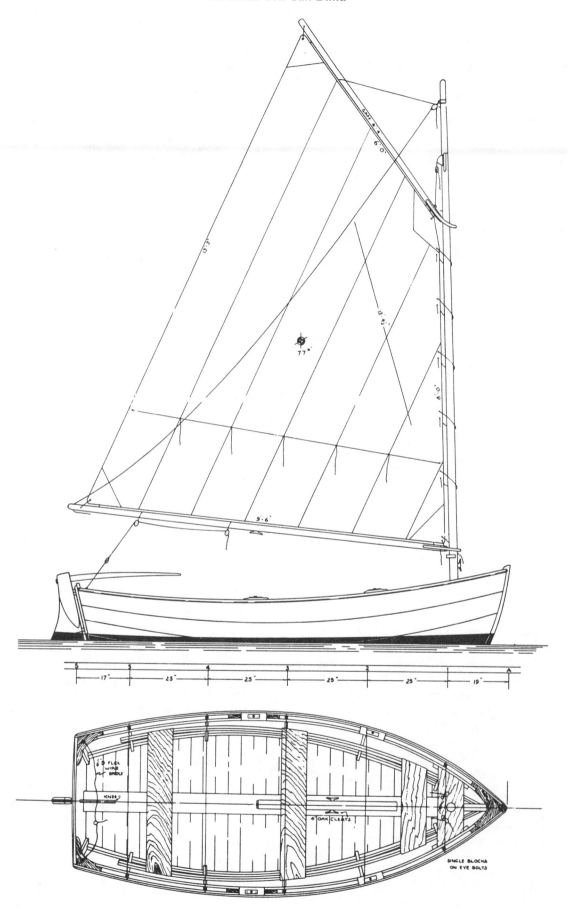

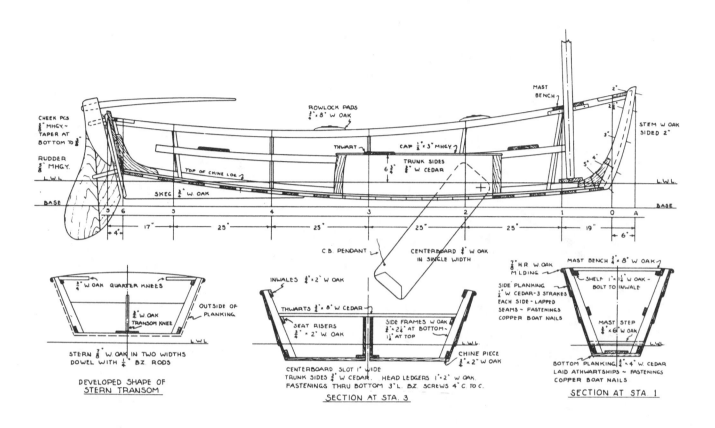

DEVELOPED SHAPE OF
STERN TRANSOM

SECTION AT STA. 3

SECTION AT STA 1

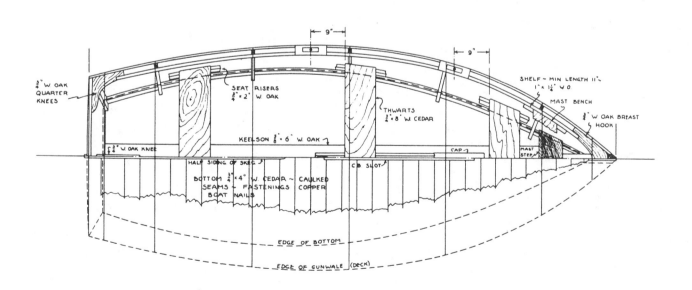

2

Elon Jessup

Length Overall: 16 feet 6 ⅜ inches
Length on Waterline: 15 feet
Beam: 5 feet 4½ inches
Draft: 6½ inches
Designer: John Atkin

A somewhat similar design to *Nina* (design No. 1) is the skiff *Elon Jessup*. Both are clinker-built, flat-bottomed boats with handsome sheerlines, designed by John Atkin, and both are relatively easy and inexpensive to build. Yet there are obvious differences: *Elon Jessup,* named after a friend of Atkin, is 6 feet longer, and she is an outboard motorboat rather than a sailing skiff. Her different function allows spacious stern sheets aft and more room forward as a result of her wide, flaring bow and lack of centerboard.

The flare is very important on *Elon Jessup,* because she naturally moves faster than *Nina* and the outward slant of her sides forward helps keep spray out of the boat. Even though her designer intended her to move at a good clip, he doesn't advise pushing her at a speed faster than about 17 m.p.h. He recommends a 10-to-12-h.p. motor. He also suggests using a long tiller so that she can be steered from the midships thwart. This keeps the weight forward, preventing the stern from dragging and the bow from lifting too high and exposing a lot of flat bottom that would pound in a chop.

Like *Nina, Elon Jessup* can be rowed, and there are two rowing positions to keep the boat in proper trim regardless of her number of passengers. As a long-time sailor with questionable mechanical abilities, I like the idea of secondary propulsion for any powerboat.

Plans from Practical Small Boat Designs *by John Atkin, International Marine, 1983*

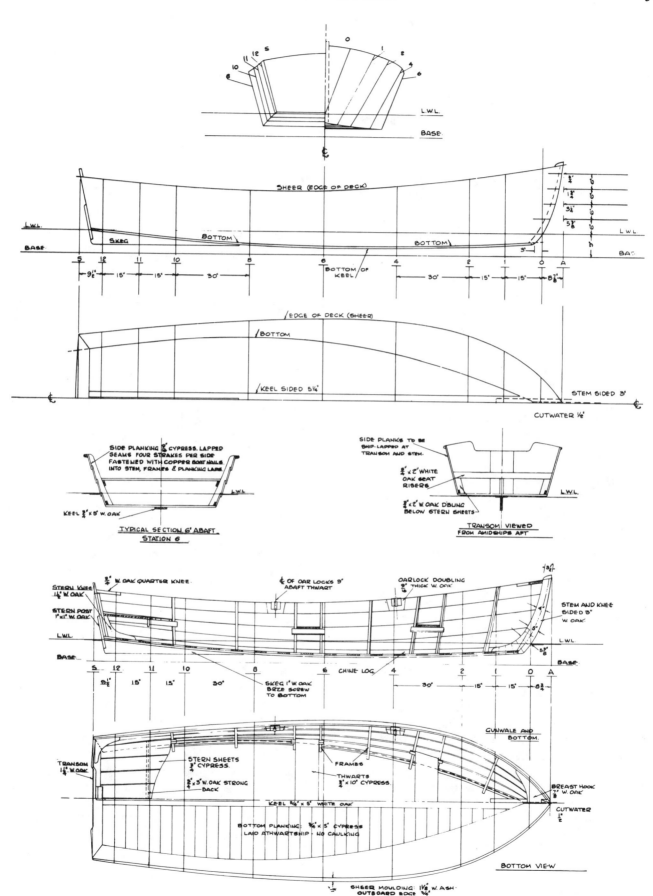

3

Valgerda

Length Overall: 18 feet 7 inches
Length on Waterline: 14 feet 9 inches
Beam: 5 feet 8 inches
Draft: 1 foot 11 inches
Displacement: 600 pounds
Sail Area: 72 square feet
Designer: John Atkin

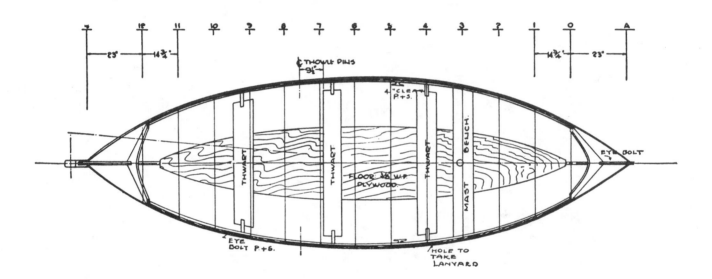

The outstanding characteristic of *Valgerda* is her lovely curvaceous shape. With her sweeping sheer, double-ended hull, turned-up ends, and handsome outboard rudder, her viking heritage is easily recognizable. She is based on a type known as a Hardangersjekte, originating in the Hardangerfjord in Norway. Her designer, John Atkin, has simplified the sectional shape to allow easy double-chine construction in mahogany plywood, and if finished bright, the boat would be strikingly beautiful.

In her workboat form, this boat has been used primarily for fishing and is quite tender when not loaded with catch. For this reason, Atkin gave her a shoal-draft ballast keel, which adds considerably to her reserve stability. I would want to add enough flotation under the thwarts and elsewhere to counteract the weight of the keel for assurance against sinking or deep swamping.

Valgerda has a simple standing lug rig that is advantageous in allowing a very short mast, a single halyard,

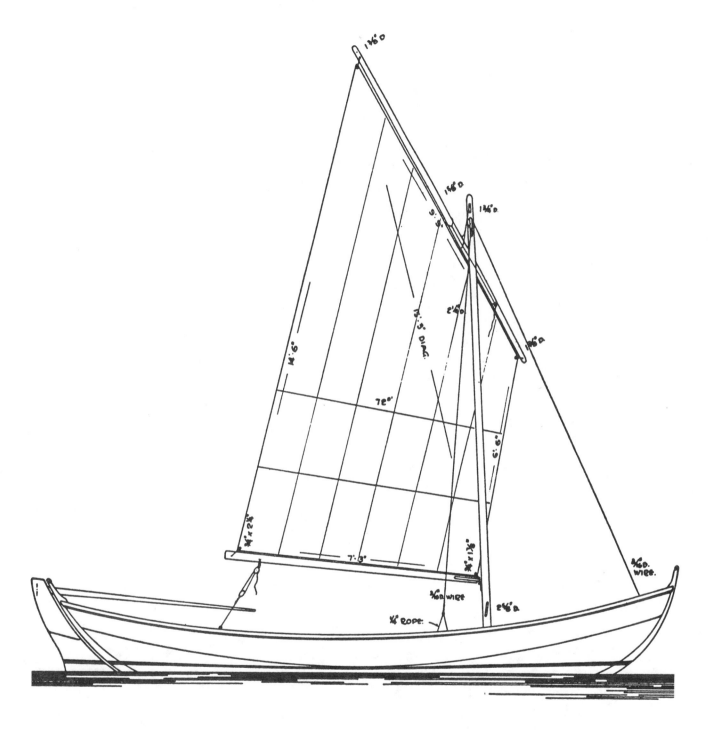

and some sail area on each side of the mast for balance when running. The standing lug rig is easier to tack than the dipping lug rig, but the mast will cut into the sail on one tack. *Valgerda* should do well on a reach or run, but I wouldn't expect too much from her windward performance. She will row well, however, and the mast can be unstepped without much trouble to reduce windage when rowing against the wind.

Plans from Practical Small Boat Designs *by John Atkin, International Marine, 1983*

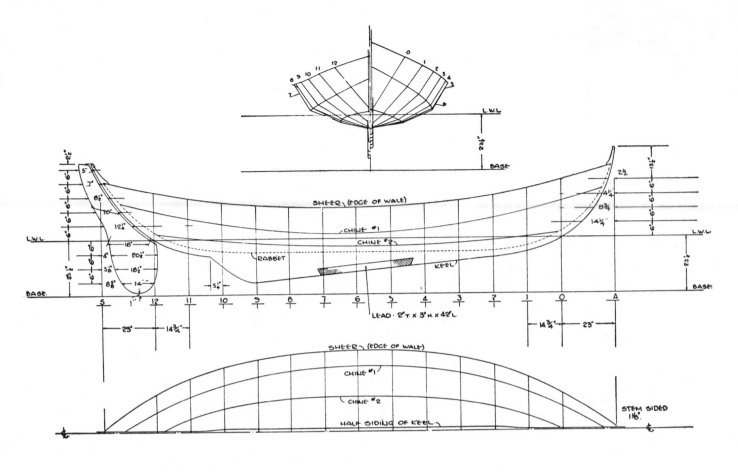

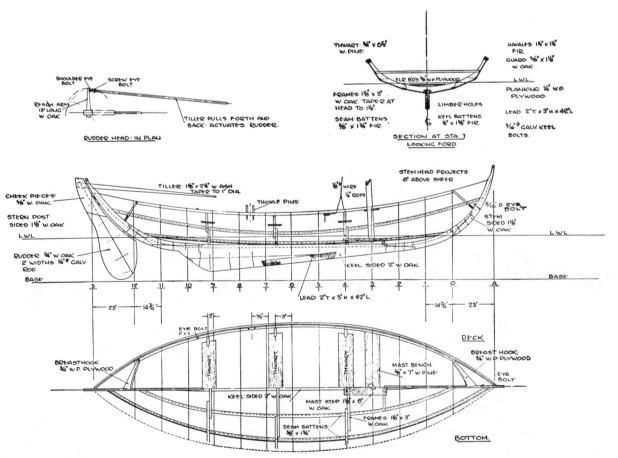

4

Amos Brown

Length on Deck: 22 feet 4¾ inches
Length on Waterline: 20 feet
Beam: 7 feet 8 inches
Draft: 3 feet
Ballast: 1,200 pounds
Sail Area: 326 square feet
Designer: John Atkin

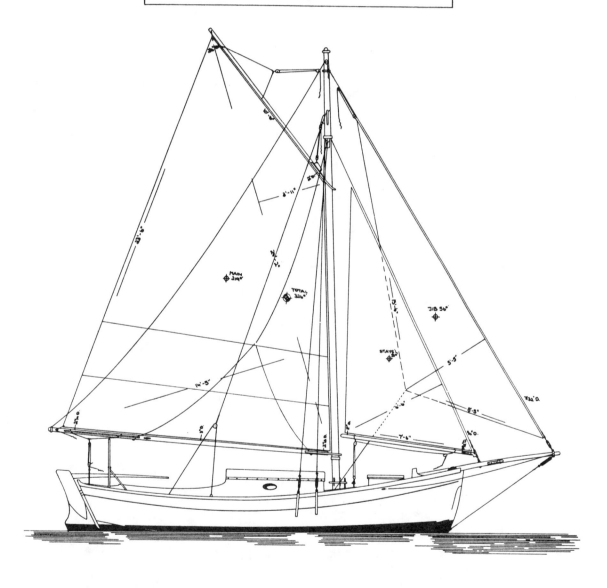

It's always interesting to see boat plans a designer produces without the influence of a client. John Atkin says that he turned out plans for the 22-foot cutter *Amos Brown* just for fun.

She is an able-looking tabloid cruiser with great character. The hefty construction, springy sheer, and certain details such as the gallows frame, outside chainplates, bitts, and pinrail give her a salty ap-

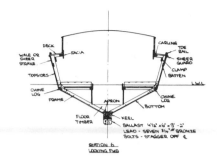

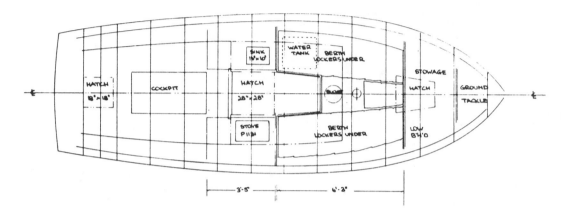

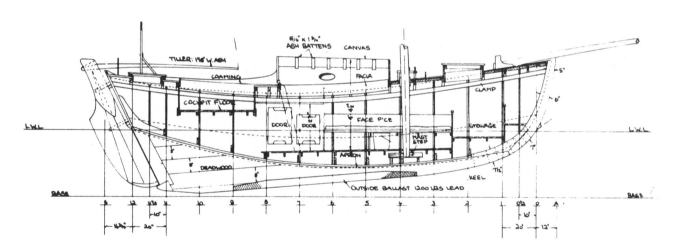

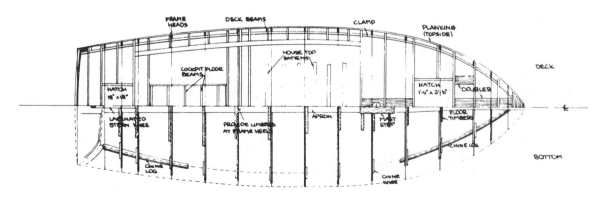

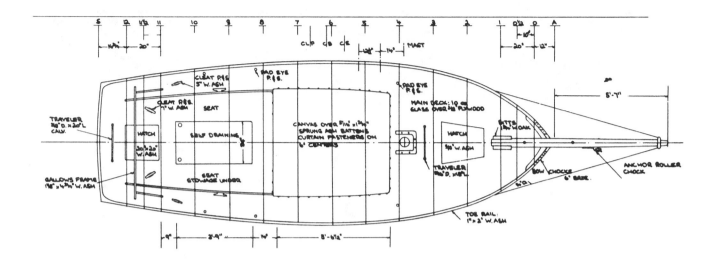

pearance. An unusual feature is the cabintop, which consists of sprung ash battens covered with removable canvas. Although you must be careful not to step on a vulnerable part of the cabintop, the arrangement enables a low, good-looking cabinhouse with plenty of headroom in good weather when the canvas is removed (the sky's the limit). *Amos Brown* has some seagoing features such as the self-bailing cockpit and the bridge deck, but the cabintop and her small size bode against any ambitious voyaging far offshore.

Despite her backstays and gaff mainsail, the rig is not too difficult to handle, because the staysail is inboard and self-tending. She seems to have plenty of sail to move well in most conditions.

You can't expect much in the way of accommodations in this size boat, but there is a good galley, two comfortable berths, and plenty of stowage space. Her deep-vee hull form simplifies construction so that a skillful amateur can build her.

Plans from Practical Small Boat Designs *by John Atkin, International Marine, 1983*

WILLIAM ATKIN

5

Mabel

Length: 10 feet
Beam: 3 feet 8 inches
Draft: 3½ inches
Weight: 100 pounds
Designer: William Atkin

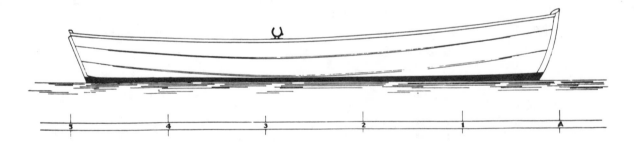

There's nothing like a flat-bottomed rowboat for honest, practical value. Here is a very special one, in fact a classic of this simple type, named *Mabel.* William Atkin, the father of John, drew her plans in 1924. Since then, these plans have appeared in numerous publications, and the blueprints have been ordered from all over the United States and many other parts of the world. A lengthy write-up of the skiff with details of her easy construction appears in *The Book of Boats,* edited by William and John Atkin.

With her curved stem, well-raked transom, graceful sheer, and lapstrake construction, *Mabel* is a lot prettier than your average flat-bottomed skiff. Like any boat of this type, she has a lot of initial stability, but also some reserve stability due to the nicely flared topsides. She is also a lot lighter than many a skiff, only about 100 pounds, and this helps make her easy to row. A good feature is the rowing foot stop that is adjustable to suit a rower of any size. The stern has plenty of buoyancy for a couple of passengers aft, and notice how the stern sheets are slotted to allow good drainage. The fairly high bow helps keep spray where it belongs even if a passenger sits forward.

The noted designer and writer Weston Farmer once said of *Mabel,* "You could call her a little workboat or just a son of a gun of a good dinghy."

Plans from The Book of Boats, *edited by William and John Atkin, International Marine, 1976*

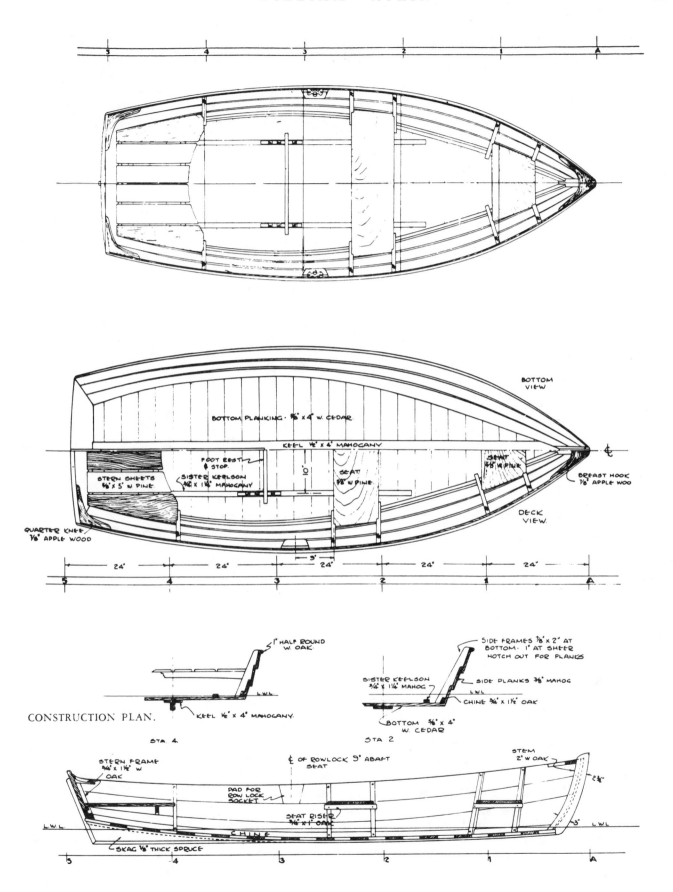

BOTTOM
VIEW

BOTTOM PLANKING · 5⁄8" x 4" W. CEDAR.

KEEL ½" X 4" MAHOGANY

FOOT REST
& STOP.

SISTER KEELSON
3⁄4" x 1¼" MAHOGANY

SEAT
7⁄8" W. PINE.

SEAT
7⁄8" W. PINE

STERN SHEETS
5⁄8" x 5" W. PINE.

BREAST HOOK
7⁄8" APPLE WOO

DECK
VIEW.

QUARTER KNEE
7⁄8" APPLE WOOD

24'   24'   3'   24'   24'

CONSTRUCTION PLAN.

1" HALF ROUND
W. OAK.

KEEL ½" X 4" MAHOGANY.

STA. 4.

SIDE FRAMES 3⁄8" X 2" AT
BOTTOM · 1" AT SHEER
NOTCH OUT FOR PLANKS

SISTER KEELSON
3⁄4" X 1¼" MAHOG

SIDE PLANKS 7⁄8" MAHOG

CHINE 3⁄4" X 1½" OAK

BOTTOM 5⁄8" X 4"
W. CEDAR

STA 2

STERN FRAME
3⁄4" X 1½" W.
OAK

¢ OF ROWLOCK 9" ABAFT
SEAT

STEM
2" W OAK

PAD FOR
ROW LOCK
SOCKET

SEAT RISER
3⁄4" X 1" OAK

CHINE

SKAG 7⁄8" THICK SPRUCE

L.W.L.

L.W.L.

6

Retreat

Length on Deck: 18 feet
Length on Waterline: 14 feet
Beam: 7 feet
Draft: 5 inches
Displacement: 1 ton
Designer: William Atkin

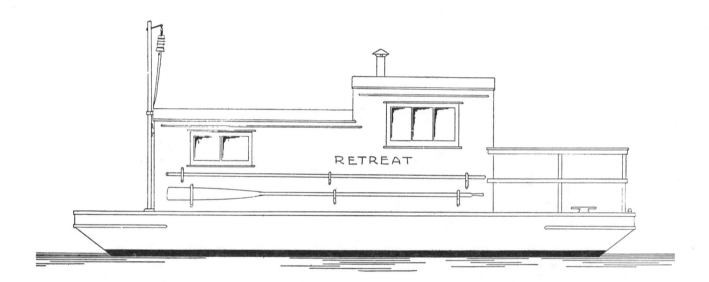

About the cheapest way to live afloat is in a small houseboat or "shantyboat deluxe," as designer William Atkin called his creation *Retreat*. In 1944 he said this 18-footer could be built for $200. We know she'd cost a lot more than that today, but she'd still be inexpensive and fairly easy for almost anyone to build. She's plain looking but practical, and her appearance is helped by the different levels of house top and "porch" railing.

The accommodations are fine for one person. Although there is not standing headroom in the sleeping area, a person 6 feet tall can stand in the galley and sitting area. There is room for chairs on the porch, where you'd spend plenty of time in fair weather. With her identical ends, you could anchor from either one bow or the other, exposing the porch to the breeze in hot weather or sheltering it in cold weather.

Of course, *Retreat* is intended for still, protected waters, and she'd be ideal for shallow creeks. You could put her where no deep-draft boats can go. You'd have privacy and a better view than a great many luxury homes. In most cases she could be propelled by an oar or a quant (note how each is stowed on the house side). Atkin even envisioned moving the boat on wheels and towing her behind a car to change to a distant locale.

Although this craft is not as richly named as the notorious Potomac River houseboat-of-ill-repute, *Aquatic Temptations,* I think *Retreat*'s name is most appropriate. She enables you to take an inexpensive breather and back off temporarily from the stress of living ashore.

Plans from The Fourth Book of Good Boats *by Roger C. Taylor, International Marine, 1984*

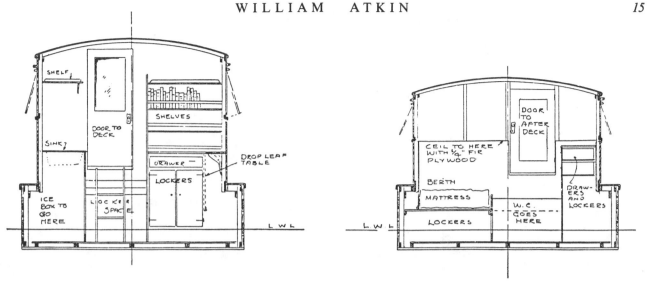

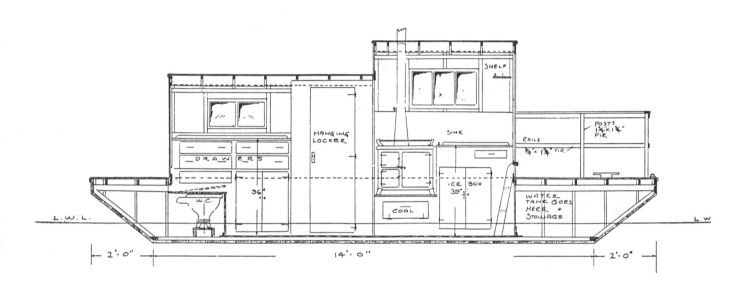

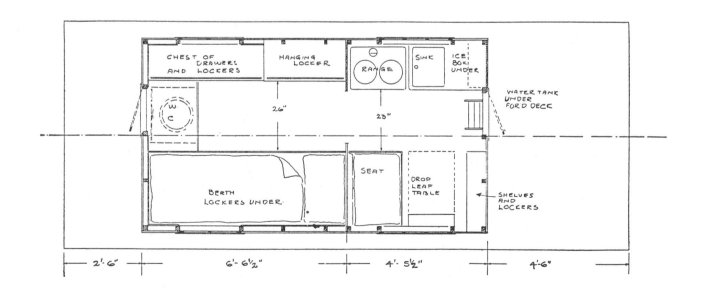

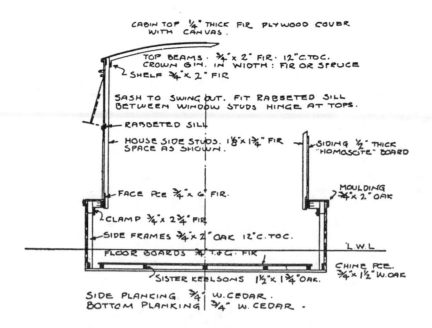

CABIN TOP ¼" THICK FIR PLYWOOD COVER
WITH CANVAS.

TOP BEAMS. ¾" X 2" FIR. 12" C.TOC.
CROWN 6IN. IN WIDTH : FIR OR SPRUCE

SHELF ¾" X 2" FIR

SASH TO SWING OUT. FIT RABBETED SILL
BETWEEN WINDOW STUDS. HINGE AT TOPS.

RABBETED SILL

HOUSE SIDE STUDS. 1⅛" X 1¾" FIR
SPACE AS SHOWN.

SIDING ½" THICK
"HOMOSOTE" BOARD

MOULDING
¾" X 2" OAK

FACE PCE ¾" X 6" FIR.

CLAMP ¾" X 2¾" FIR

SIDE FRAMES ¾" X 2" OAK 12" C.TOC.

L.W.L.

FLOOR BOARDS ¾" T.&G. FIR

CHINE PCE.
¾" X 1½" W.OAK

SISTER KEELSONS 1½" X 1¾" OAK.

SIDE PLANKING ¾" W. CEDAR .
BOTTOM PLANKING ¾" W. CEDAR .

SECTION AT MAIN CABIN

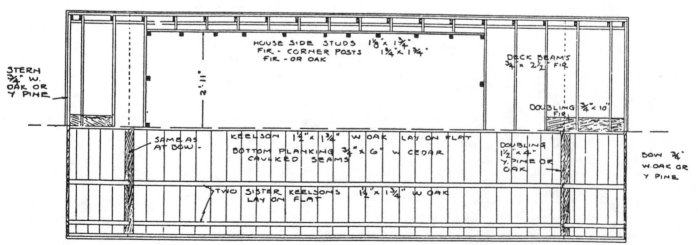

DECK TWO THICKNESSES
OF ¼" FIR PLYWOOD
COVER WITH CANVAS

HOUSE SIDES AND ENDS ½" THICK
"HOMOSOTE" BOARD

MOULDING
¾" X 2"
OAK

CLAMP ¾" X 2¾" FIR.

SIDE FRAMES ¾" X 2" W OAK   12" C TO C

L.W.L.

CHINE PCS ¾" X 1½" W OAK

L.W.L.

2'·0"

BOTTOM   14' LONG

2'·0"

HOUSE SIDE STUDS 1⅛" X 1¾"
FIR - CORNER POSTS   1¼" X 1¾"
FIR - OR OAK

DECK BEAM'S
¾" X 2½" FIR

STERN
¾" W.
OAK OR
Y PINE

2'·11"

DOUBLING ¾" X 10"
FIR

SAME AS
AT BOW.

KEELSON 1½" X 1¾" W OAK LAY ON FLAT

BOTTOM PLANKING ¾" X 6" W CEDAR
CAULKED SEAMS

DOUBLING
1½" X 4"
Y. PINE OR
OAK

BOW ¾"
W.OAK OR
Y PINE

TWO SISTER KEELSONS   1½" X 1¾" W OAK
LAY ON FLAT

7

Sabot

Length on Deck: 19 feet 6 inches
Length on Waterline: 16 feet
Beam: 6 feet 4 inches
Draft: 3 feet
Displacement: 3,450 pounds
Sail Area: 189 square feet
Designer: William Atkin

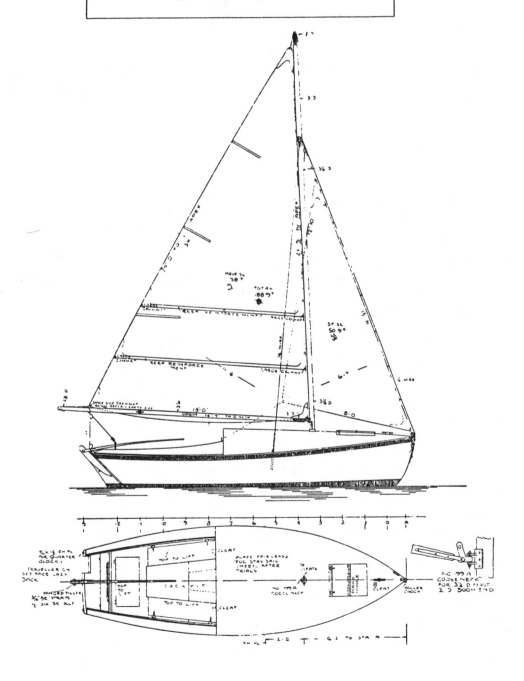

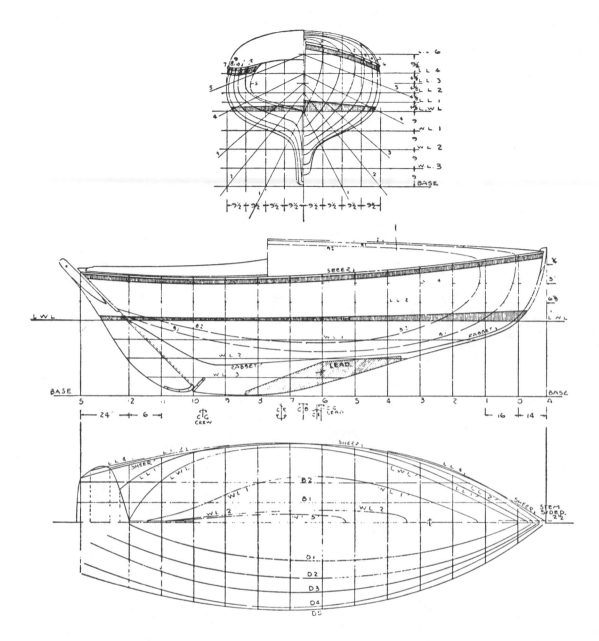

Not everyone likes the looks of a turtleback cabinhouse, but it affords a lot of room below and adds greatly to the strength of the boat. This little 19-foot cruiser named *Sabot* is particularly strong; her scantlings are hefty, her hull shape is round, and she has no companionway hatch to break the curved deckbeams.

William Atkin designed *Sabot* in 1934 for a well-known yachtsman, Elihu Root, Jr. (inventor of the Root berth). She evolved from a 20-foot singlehander named *Dormouse* that Atkin, together with Starling Burgess, designed for Root several years earlier. *Dormouse* was unusual in that she was a shoal-draft keelboat with exceptional windward ability, so it would not be surprising if *Sabot* also performs well close-hauled. This seems to be verified by her fairly fine lines, effective salient keel, low wetted surface area, and slope of the keel, which allows a long leading edge to cut solid water. With her generous waterline beam and 45 percent ballast ratio, *Sabot* should be amply stiff.

The rig is small and handy. Although the single shroud led far aft prevents squaring the boom when running, the simple "three-stay" rig obviates the need for running backstays.

Sabot was intended for cool climes (note the heating stove), and the cabin could be a bit cavelike in hot regions. A couple of small oval ports and low deck ventilators might be in order. Also, you might want to add a couple of toe rails on the turtleback. The cockpit is not self-bailing, but its deep foot well affords great protection and security.

Plans from Still More Good Boats *by Roger C. Taylor, International Marine, 1981*

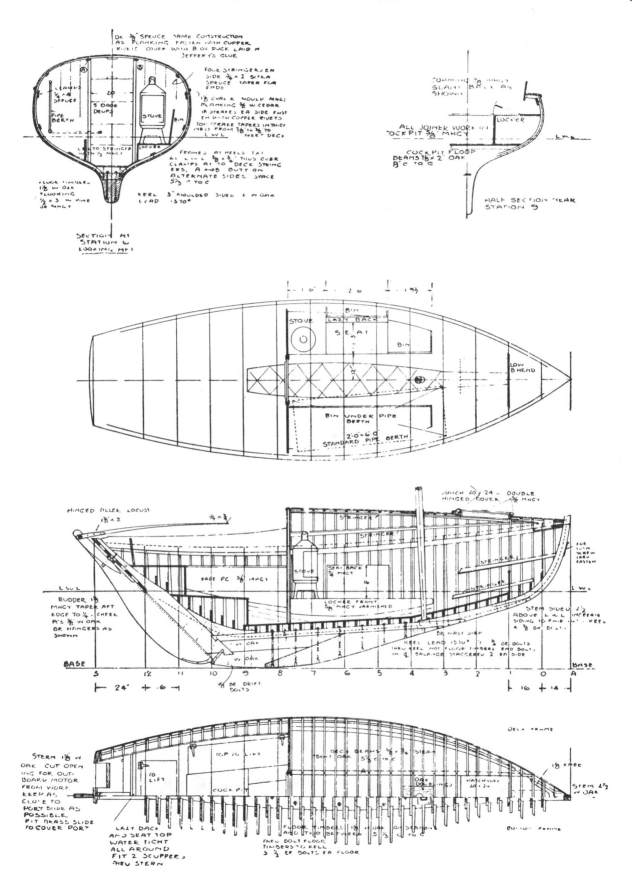

8

Shore Liner

Length on Deck: 24 feet
Length on Waterline: 22 feet
Beam: 9 feet
Draft: 1 foot
Sail Area: 365 square feet
Designers: William and John Atkin

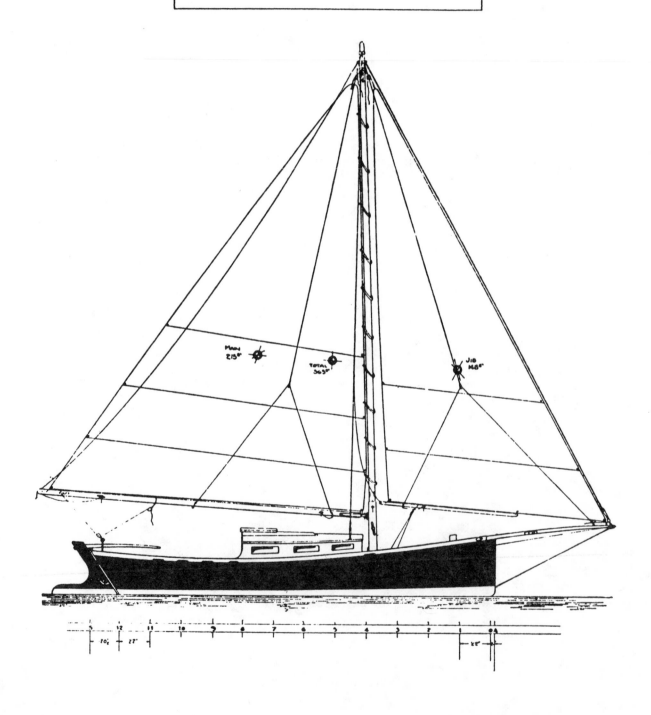

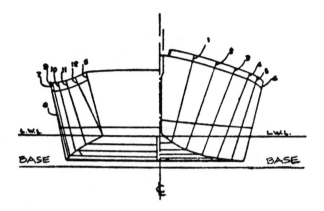

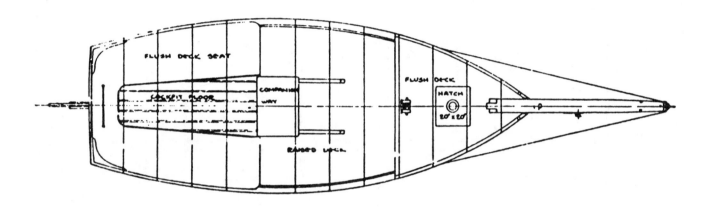

Shore Liner is a square-sterned sharpie type that William and John Atkin designed from preliminary plans by Ed Hanks. The main advantages of the type are easy and inexpensive construction, high initial stability, and shoal draft. With her centerboard up, *Shore Liner* draws only a foot of water. Disadvantages of a sharpie include susceptibility to some pounding in head seas, a low range of stability, and a lack of bilge depth, which takes away headroom and creates a problem with bilge water.

Because she can capsize, *Shore Liner* has been given a low-aspect-ratio rig, and it is good that she has plenty of reef points. Still, there is a lot of sail area spread out longitudinally, and the boat should have all the power she needs for speed on a run or reach. I would not expect her to be very close-winded, but she should be capable of reasonable progress to windward.

Her cockpit is roomy, and there are adequate accommodations below for two. With her raised-deck cabin, there is more room below than the plans indicate, although there is only 48 inches of headroom. An unusual feature for such a small boat are the seats, which are used only for seats.

You couldn't call *Shore Liner* a beautiful boat, but she has a certain character. Coming from the Chesapeake, I might want to add a curved cutwater and trail boards to make her resemble a skipjack.

Obviously, *Shore Liner* is not an offshore boat, but she is a fine, inexpensive gunkholer, and as Hanks said, "She isn't just another sailboat — she is a cocky little hooker."

Plans from The Book of Boats, *edited by William and John Atkin, International Marine, 1976*

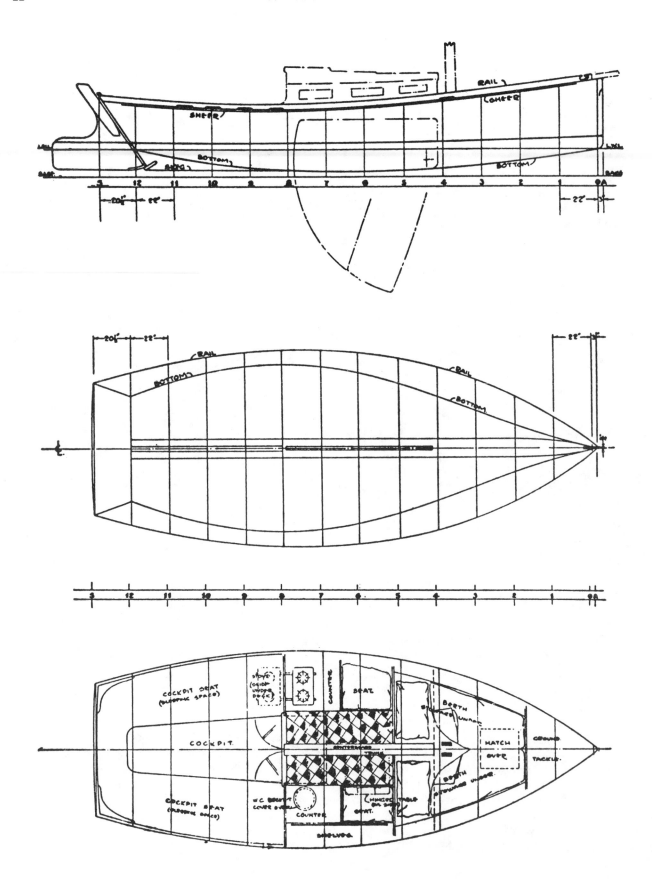

9

Fair Wind

Length on Deck: 26 feet 5 inches
Length on Waterline: 21 feet 6 inches
Beam: 9 feet 6 inches
Draft: 3 feet
Sail Area: 349 square feet
Designer: William Atkin

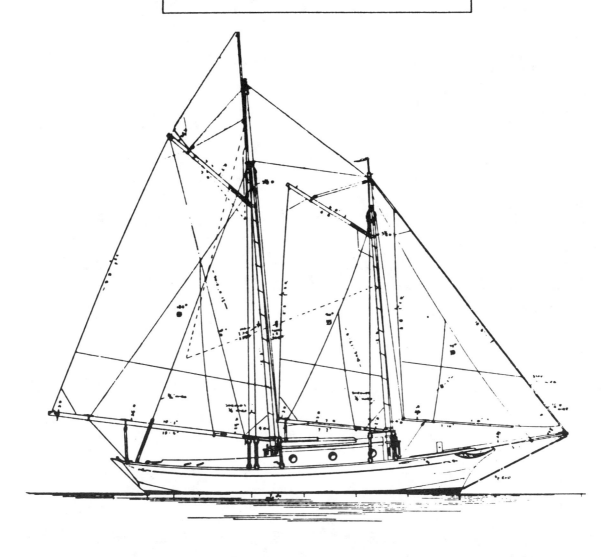

Any boat with chines and hard bilges is apt to pound at times, but the type least likely to slam is a rather deep-vee hull, as exemplified by the William Atkin–designed schooner *Fair Wind*. Her sectional form is not unlike that of the famous Sea Bird yawls that made so many offshore passages. Although I wouldn't recommend *Fair Wind* for offshore voyaging with her centerboard and fairly low range of stability, she'd be a fine coastal or shallow-water cruiser, and she might be faster than a Sea Bird with the moderate rocker in her chine, long waterline, and generous sailplan. Having a longer keel, she'd probably self-steer a bit better than a Sea Bird.

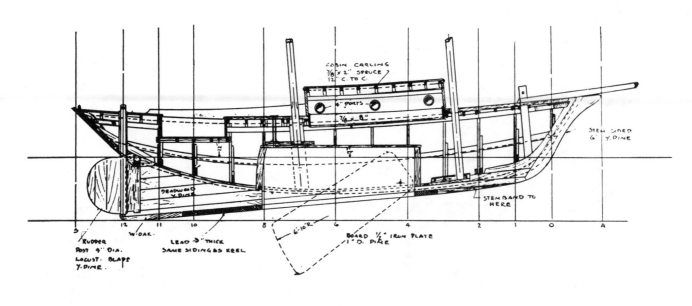

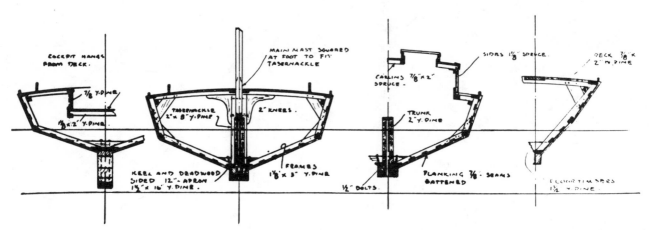

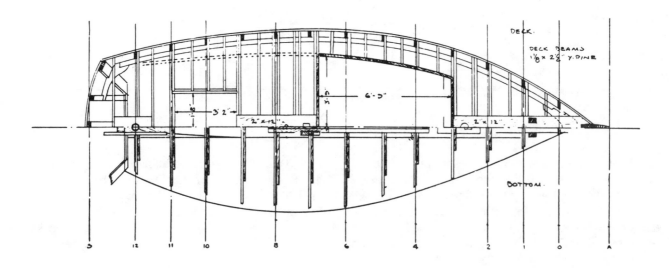

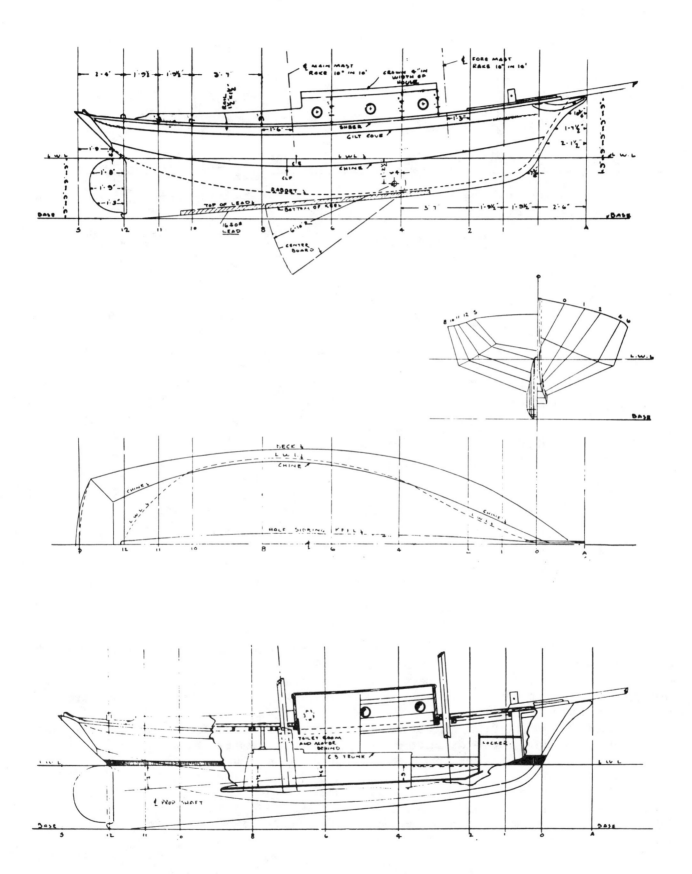

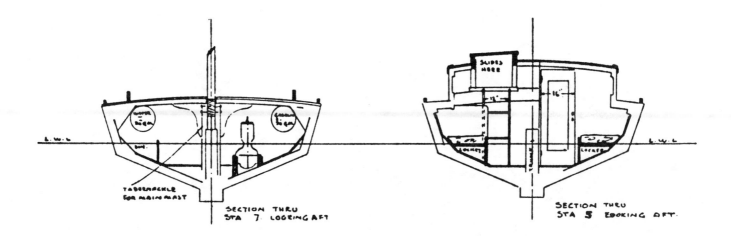

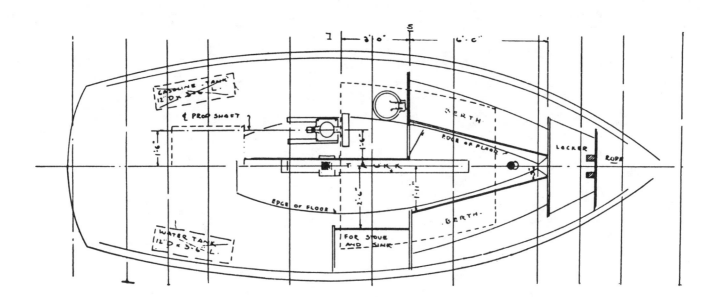

Considering the fact that she's only 26 feet long and has heavy, space-robbing construction, a short cabin trunk, and a centerboard well, *Fair Wind* has surprisingly good accommodations for two. Even if the bunks are narrow, the head is enclosed, and there is space for a practical galley. The cockpit well is small for safety and drainage, but there is plenty of room to sit on deck. And what an expanse of bridge deck for sunbathing and sleeping in fair weather!

The schooner rig affords a low aspect ratio and spread-out sail area, which are advantageous for stability and balance. The considerable rake of her masts probably obviates the need for using the running backstays except in a fresh breeze and when hard on the wind.

Fair Wind is a distinctive-looking boat with her big-boat rig, clipper bow with trail boards, strongly raked transom, bold sheer, and well-steeved bowsprit. I would want only to lower the forward end of her cabin trunk, because it makes the boat look as though she is trimmed by the stern, an illusion that is reinforced by the mast rake. I like a rakish look, but one that seems to be on the level.

Plans from The Fourth Book of Good Boats *by Roger C. Taylor, International Marine, 1984*

10

Eric

Length on Deck: 32 feet 1 inch
Length on Waterline: 27 feet 6 inches
Beam: 11 feet
Draft: 5 feet
Displacement: 9¾ tons
Sail Area: 790 square feet
Designer: William Atkin

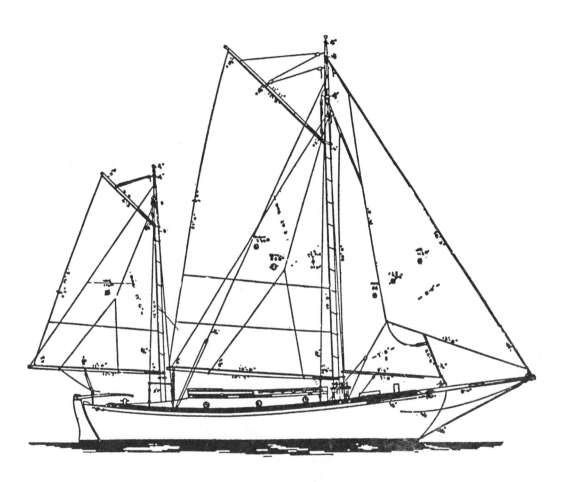

Few small craft evoke a greater feeling of security in the open sea than the Redningskoites or double-ended sailing lifeboats designed by Colin Archer. *Eric* is a small, modified version of a Redningskoite. William Atkin designed her for the noted yachtsman Bill Nutting, who was one of the founders of the Cruising Club of America. A boat of this type, *Suhaili,* was raced solo and nonstop around the world in 1968-1969 by Robin Knox-Johnson. *Suhaili* was the only boat of nine starters to finish, and she completed her antipodal circumnavigation in about 10 and a half months, which speaks well of her passagemaking and seakeeping abilities.

In my opinion, *Eric*'s lines show some improvement over the original Redningskoite in that the bow is finer for better performance against head seas, and the

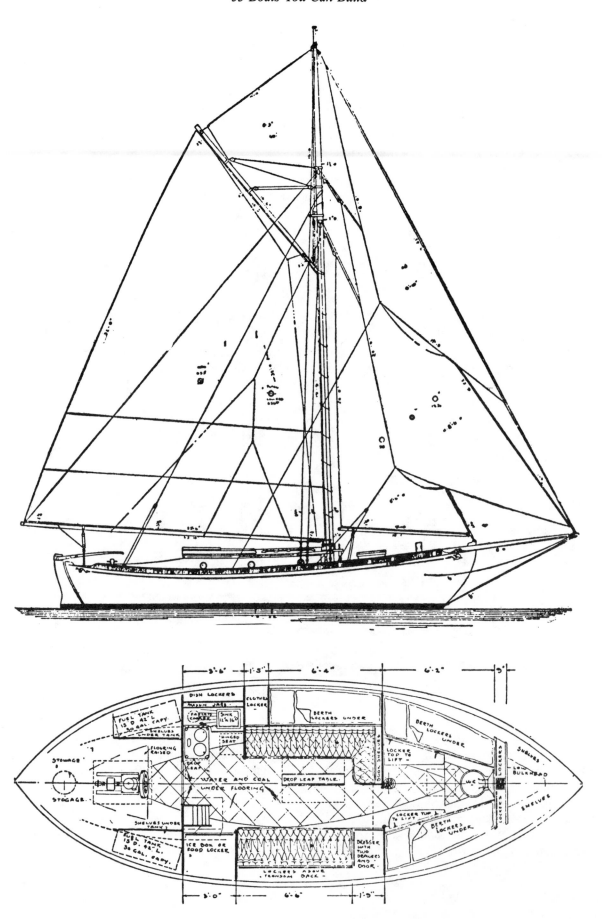

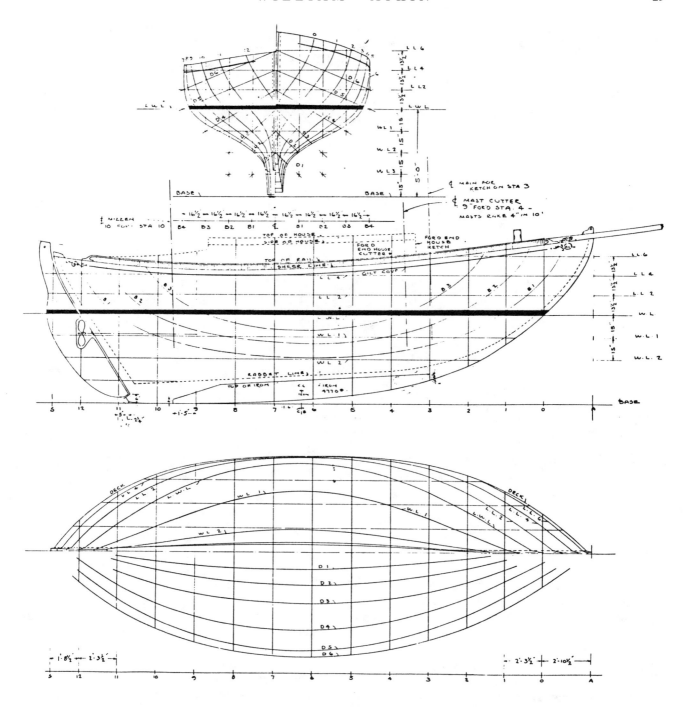

forefoot is a bit more cutaway for improved maneuverability and less wetted surface. The basic layout below is fine, except that I'd want to have an enclosed head, which would take some rearranging, perhaps sacrificing the port bunk up forward. There are sailplans for two rigs. The ketch rig would be a handier one for short-handed sailing, whereas the cutter rig would provide better performance to windward and in light airs.

Eric spent a number of years in my home waters at Gibson Island, Maryland. She was no speed demon in the Chesapeake zephyrs, but she could move well in a breeze, and her looks were always greatly admired.

Plans from Colin Archer and the Seaworthy Double-Ender *by John Leather, International Marine, 1979*

JAY BENFORD

11
Bakea

Length on Deck: 30 feet
Length on Waterline: 28 feet 6 inches
Beam: 10 feet 6 inches
Draft: 4 feet 6 inches
Sail Area: 558 square feet
Designer: Jay R. Benford

A former apprentice of John Atkin, Jay R. Benford, is a yacht designer with strong traditional roots but with many innovative ideas. Particularly imaginative are his interior layouts.

Bakea is one variation of the Benford 30, which the designer says evolved from the Friendship sloop. This heritage is hard to recognize, however, because the Benford 30 has been given much greater freeboard, a highly modified keel, and a greatly altered underbody, as well as a different rig. There are many versions of the Benford 30, *Bakea* being a pilothouse model with a great cabin aft. This model would be most suitable for northern waters, or for long cruises in warmer climes late or early in the boating season.

For a 30-footer, the accommodations are incredible. The great cabin has a huge settee that converts to three berths (I'd want to sleep aft where I could look out of the transom ports) and a drop-leaf table; the adjoining pilothouse has a splendid galley, chart table, enclosed head, and steering station. Up forward there is a double berth, single berth, and another head. Would you believe there's still room for a sizable engine room?

One might think *Bakea* would lack stability with her top hamper, but a Benford stability curve shows that the Benford 30 has positive stability to over 120 degrees (better than many IOR boats). She sails well for her type, and her designer claims that she actually excels to windward. The rig is easy to handle, and there is an outside steering station even if it is a bit far forward.

Although she was intended for fiberglass construction, *Bakea* can be built of other materials. She is a versatile boat with considerable character and unbelievable room.

Plans from Cruising Yachts *by Jay R. Benford, 1983*

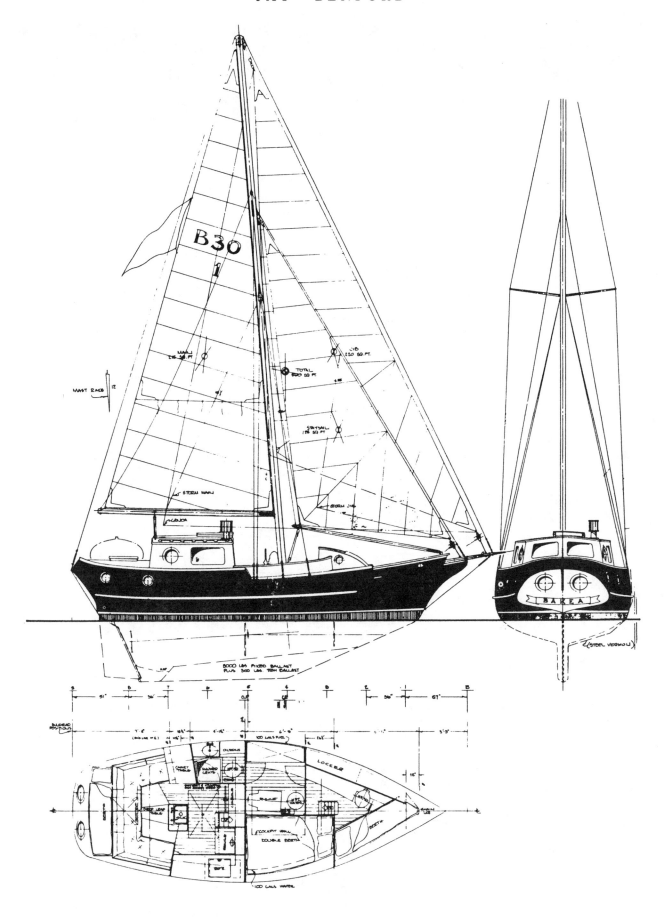

PHILIP C. BOLGER

12

The Elegant Punt

Length: 7 feet 9 inches
Beam: 3 feet 7 inches
Weight: 70 pounds
Sail Area: 59 square feet
Designer: Philip C. Bolger

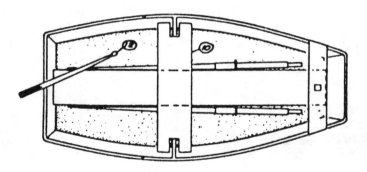

One of the most individualistic of contemporary yacht designers is Philip C. Bolger of Gloucester, Massachusetts. He questions and often disagrees with the sailing establishment and frequently produces designs that are offbeat. Judging from the names he gives some of his designs — *Kotik, Mippet, Prancing Pony,* and *Bird of Dawning* — he is a litterateur and a romantic. Despite this (or because of it), he has turned out some very practical and logical boats that have character and can be produced inexpensively.

About the simplest, cheapest, and easiest boat to build next to a scow is the punt, especially when it is a small one like this sailing model Bolger designed. The punt is a development and improvement over the scow in that the bottom is rockered, the topsides are flared, and the bow is raked. I like to see the bow well raked so that the boat will not be stopped by choppy seas. *The Elegant Punt* uses only one leeboard for lateral resistance. Keeping the board on one side causes the boat to have about the same loss of efficiency on either

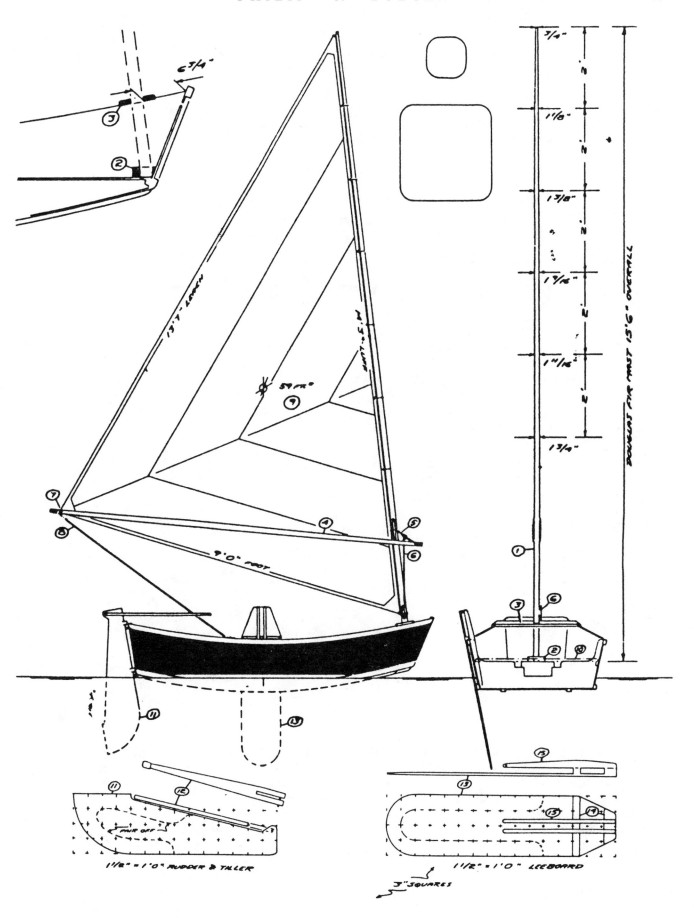

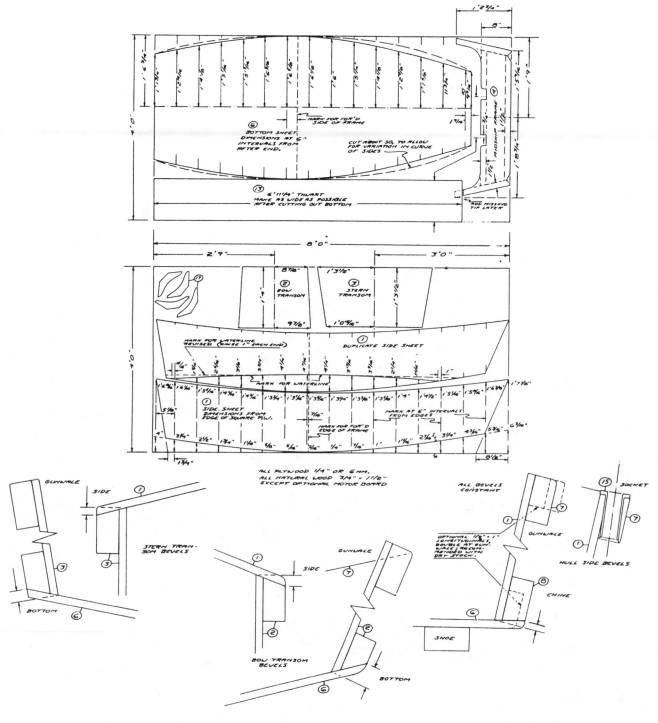

tack. On the low side, the board angles away from the vertical. On the high side, the board has less draft but a more vertical angle.

She carries a lot of sail, and the designer says she sails better than you might expect. The sprit boom is a nice feature, as it allows shaping the sail and keeps the boom up high. Bolger implies that she doesn't row or tow

quite as well as she sails. With her efficient rig, springy sheer, well-rockered bottom, and businesslike rudder, this boat might indeed be considered elegant for an 8-foot punt.

Plans from The Fourth Book of Good Boats *by Roger C. Taylor, International Marine, 1984*

13
Defender

Length: 11 feet
Beam: 3 feet 10 inches
Weight: 100 pounds
Designer: Philip C. Bolger

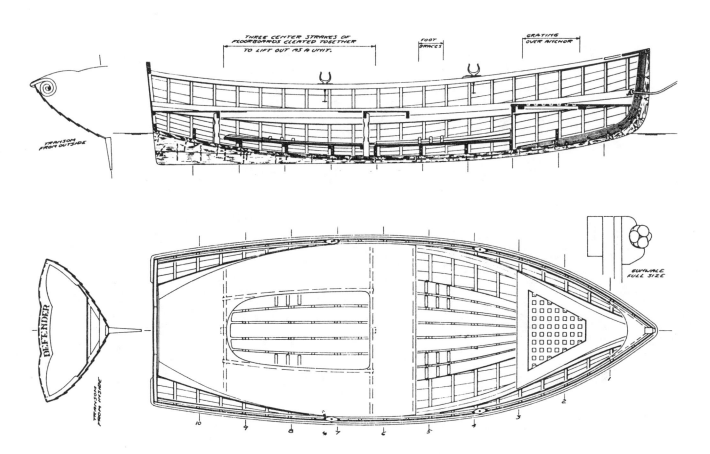

Phil Bolger says that his *Defender* design is meant to resemble an 1890-vintage yacht tender, the kind often seen hanging in side davits on medium-sized schooner yachts. She is certainly a pretty boat, with her pronounced sheer, curvaceous lower stem, hollow bow, distinctive transom, and lapstrake construction. The designer points out that many of the period yacht tenders of this type were carvel built because of their silence among ripples at night, but I prefer the lapstrakes for their watertightness and appearance. And

the lapping of ripples against a clinker-built boat is a soothing sound to me, but then I'm easily lulled asleep on a boat.

Defender is a roomy boat able to hold six people in calm weather. Despite having rather fine lines forward and aft, she has a lot of reserve buoyancy. She weighs about 140 pounds, but the designer says the weight can be reduced to about 90 pounds, with lighter, but reasonably strong, construction. An easy boat to row, *Defender* also behaves well when towed. Drag under

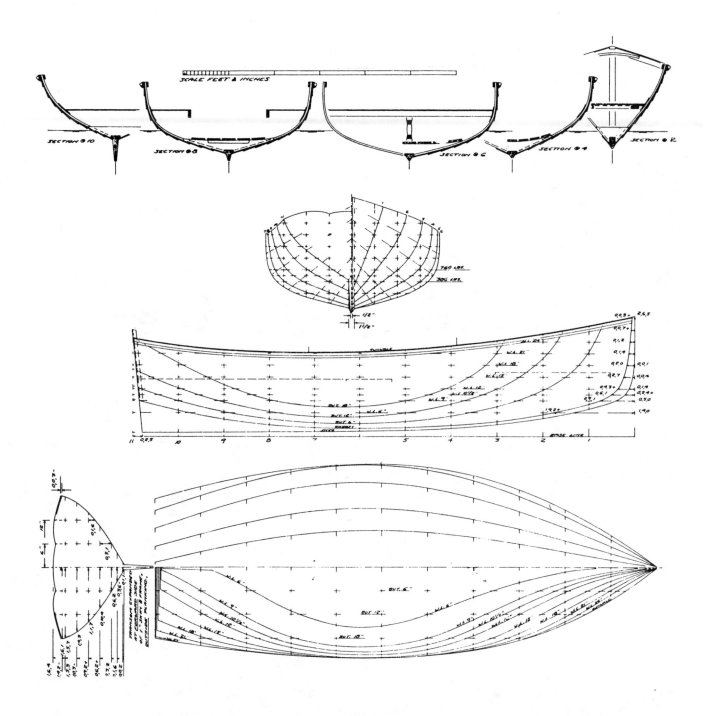

tow is minimal, and her large skeg helps prevent yawing. Given leeboards and a rudder, she can even sail well, Bolger claims. He admits, however, that she is a trifle weak in the quarters compared to the very best of the frostbiters. He suggests a pole mast (it could be in two pieces) and a sail with a generous roach held out by full-length battens.

Of course, *Defender* is primarily a pulling boat, and her suitability for rowing in a variety of loading and weather conditions is her forte. Her sailing potential could be considered a lagniappe.

Plans from Bolger Boats *by Philip C. Bolger, International Marine, 1983*

14

Teal

Length: 12 feet
Beam: 3 feet 6 inches
Sail Area: 59 square feet
Designer: Philip C. Bolger

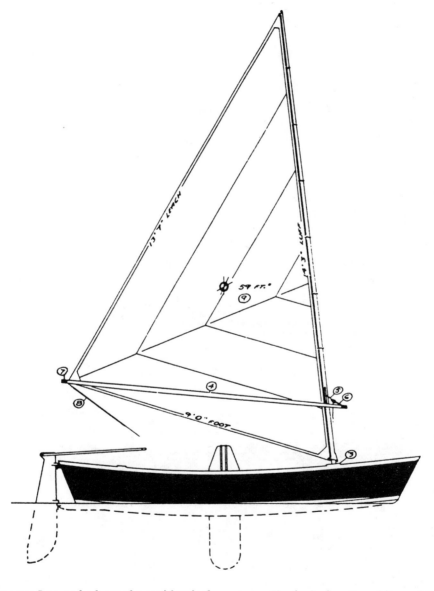

When I was a youngster I owned a boat almost identical to the Phil Bolger–designed *Teal*. I found her on a scrap heap with a missing bottom, so, with no previous experience in carpentry, I put on a new cross-planked bottom. She leaked quite a bit, and I named her *Bird of Drowning*, a takeoff on the synonym for rooster and the title of a great John Masefield book. Despite her weeps, I had much fun with the *Bird*, and she served me well as

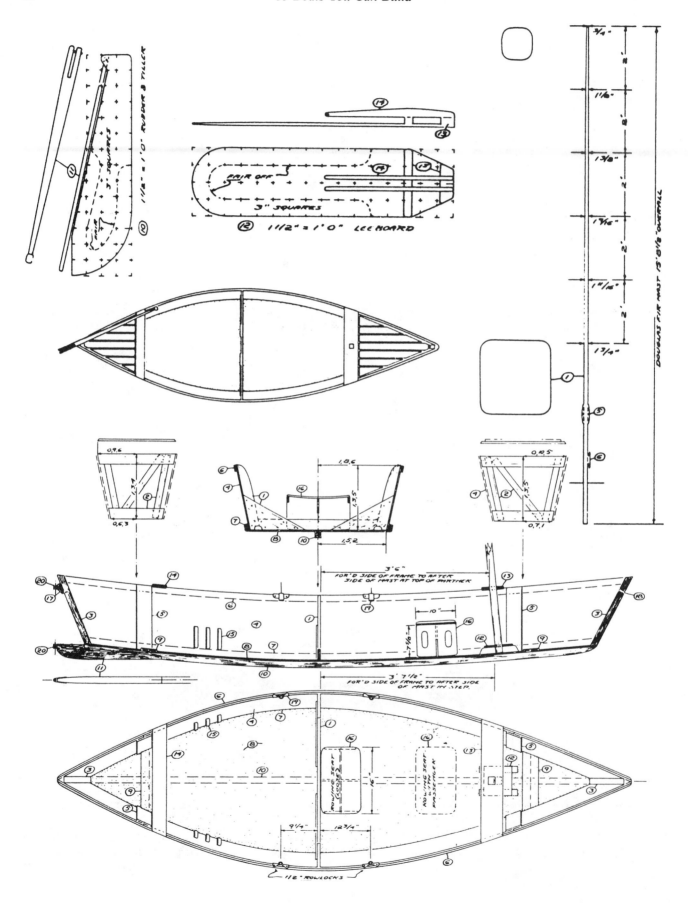

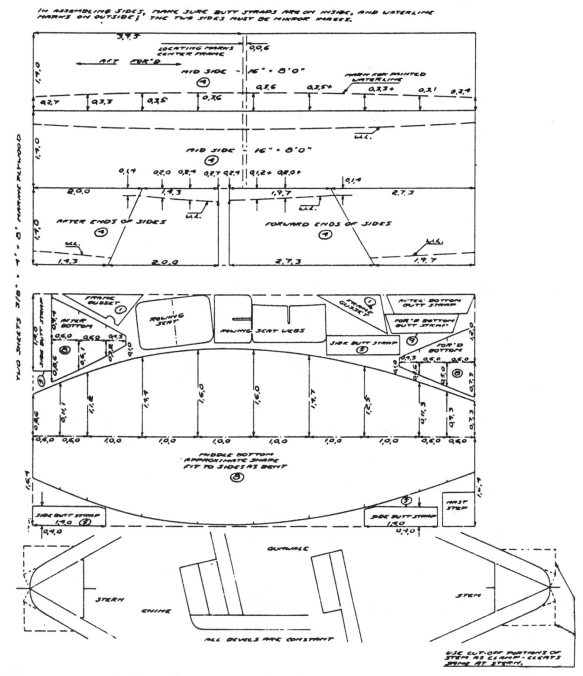

a leeboard sailer and pulling boat. With the help of a friend, I once rowed her across the Chesapeake Bay and back, a distance of 12 miles in my area.

With her plywood bottom, *Teal* should not present any leaking problems. She also has plywood topsides and is a cinch for anyone with any woodworking ability to build.

If *Teal* performs like my *Bird* — and I'm sure that if there is any difference the Bolger boat behaves better — she not only rows well, but also sails fast. The leg-o'-mutton sail with a sprit boom is generous in area and easy to handle. One might expect a flattie to pound,

but I found that if you let her heel a little, the chine cuts through the chop. Of course, you must be careful not to her her heel too much, or water will slop over the gunwale. *Teal* has a bit more freeboard than my boat had, and that is helpful.

Teal is simple, pretty, and functional for sheltered waters. One of her few foibles is a lack of load capacity, but if you recognize this limitation, she is, as Bolger put it, "a paragon of all the virtues."

Plans from Bolger Boats *by Philip C. Bolger, International Marine, 1983*

15

The Thomaston Galley

Length: 15 feet 6 inches
Beam: 4 feet 1 inch
Weight: 140 pounds
Sail Area: 71½ square feet
Designer: Philip C. Bolger

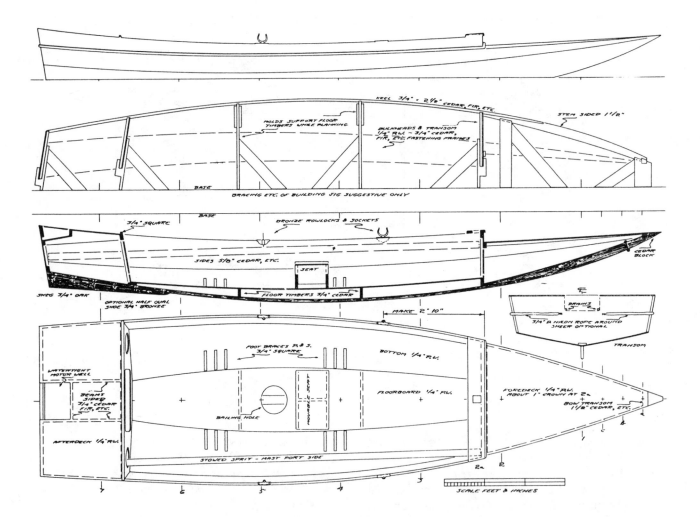

To create an inexpensive boat that performs well and is fairly fast under oars, sail, or power seems a lot to ask of a designer; this is what Phil Bolger attempted, and he pulled it off remarkably well with his 16-foot Thomaston Galley.

He produced a vee-bottomed hull that has a long bow overhang with lots of flare forward and that is very broad aft. The wide stern supplies plenty of buoyancy for an outboard motor and people aft, but the after sections are not quite as flat as some sheltered-water plan-

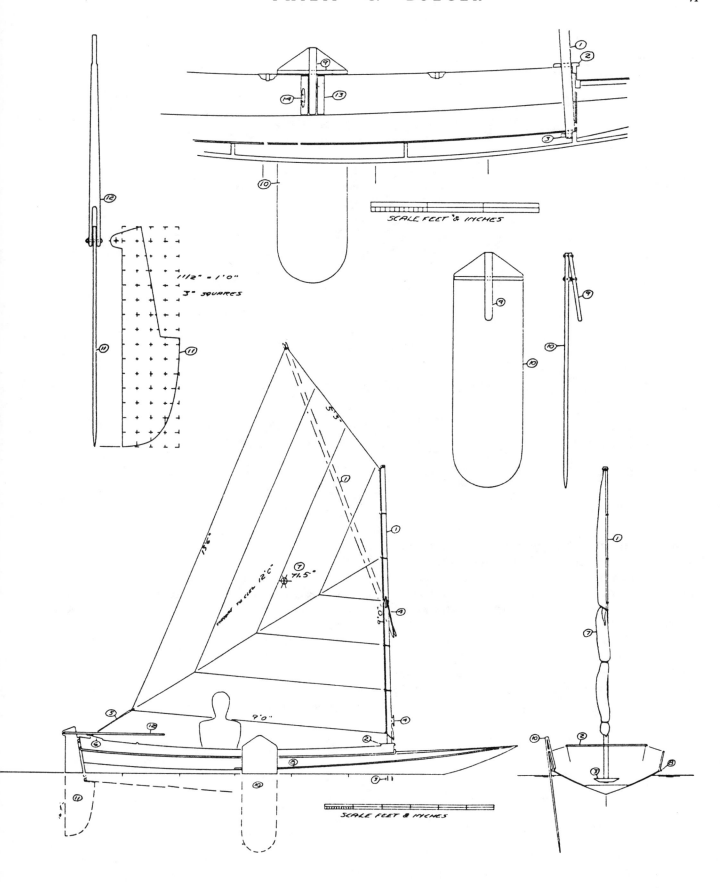

SCALE FEET & INCHES

SCALE FEET & INCHES

1 1/2" = 1'0"

3" SQUARES

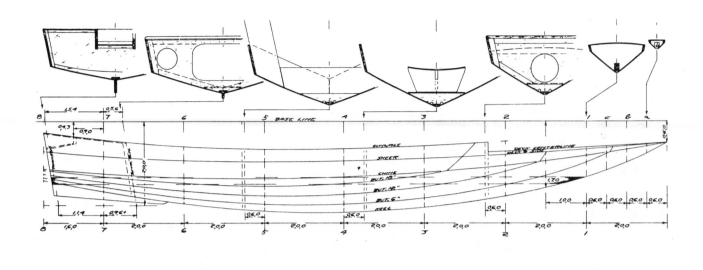

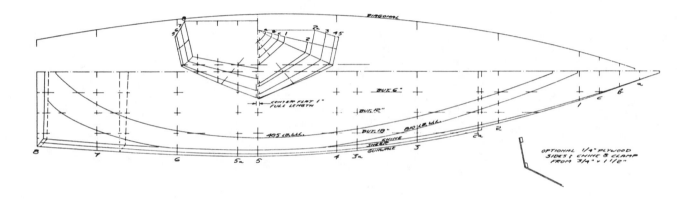

ing motorboats, which helps give the boat balance for her multiple duties. Although the bow is quite fine, the flare and overhang provide considerable reserve buoyancy forward. Freeboard is low, but the cockpit is surrounded by a high coaming that helps keep the water where it belongs.

There is a motor well aft for a small outboard and a movable rowing seat. Bolger writes that he can row her at 5½ m.p.h. for a short distance. The Galley is also fast under sail, although the designer says that she is not very close-winded. She carries one leeboard and a sprit

rig. A big advantage of the spritsail is the short spars, which can be stowed in the boat.

Although she is strictly intended for protected waters, the Thomaston Galley is a versatile little boat. Aside from her abilities afloat, she is easily trailerable, and Bolger claims that, thanks to her long bow, he can haul her up on a trailer without wetting his wheels. He admits to being proud of the design.

Plans from Bolger Boats *by Philip C. Bolger, International Marine, 1983*

16

Victoria

Length: 15 feet 6 inches
Beam: 4 feet 2 inches
Designer: Philip C. Bolger

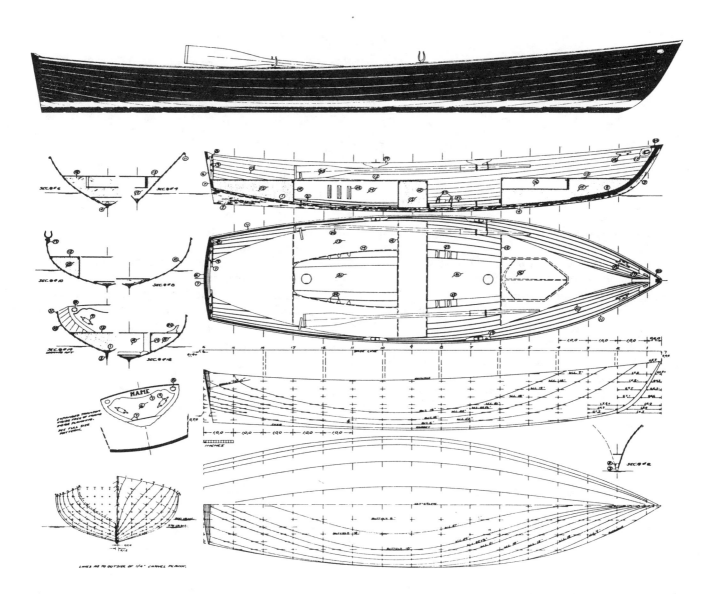

The design for *Victoria* is based on a pulling boat that Phil Bolger built while working in Spain. The Spanish-built boat was so appealing that when an article on her appeared in *Boating* magazine, Bolger says he received about 1,500 letters from readers wanting to buy her plans. *Victoria* is not quite as fancy as the Spanish boat, but she is more practical and versatile. She is light, easily trailerable, buoyant enough for carrying a small family, sufficiently stable for debarking over the bow, sturdy enough for beaching, and easily rowed.

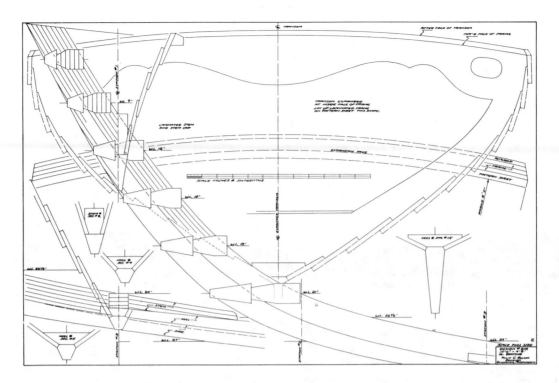

It certainly helps when the designer of a pulling boat is an experienced oarsman, and Bolger is a rowing enthusiast. He thinks that for short distances a dinghy should be propelled by oars rather than outboard motor. I certainly agree, although I don't feel quite as strongly as my father, who thought the outboard motor was a major step toward the ruination of modern man. At any rate, Bolger knew what he was doing when he designed *Victoria*. She has the length for speed, a sharp entrance to knife through a chop, flare forward for dryness, sufficient beam for stability, a clean run aft for

low drag, and a wineglass stern for reserve buoyancy and beauty. Construction is lapstrake using plywood.

The designer feels this boat is particularly suitable for two or three people, rowing one at a time. In calm weather he says it's possible to cover 30 miles in one day in this manner. This claim indicates not only that the designer is a dedicated oarsman, but also that his creation is exceedingly functional.

Plans from Bolger Boats *by Philip C. Bolger, International Marine, 1983*

17

Light Dory Type V

Length: 4.74 meters
Beam: 1.22 meters
Designer: Philip C. Bolger

There are arguments over the merits of the dory as a sea boat. The narrow-bottomed kind is extremely low in initial stability and the U.S. Coast Guard frowns on

such tenderness, but dories normally have good reserve stability. Dories have crossed the Atlantic several times, and offshore-banks fishermen have used the design suc-

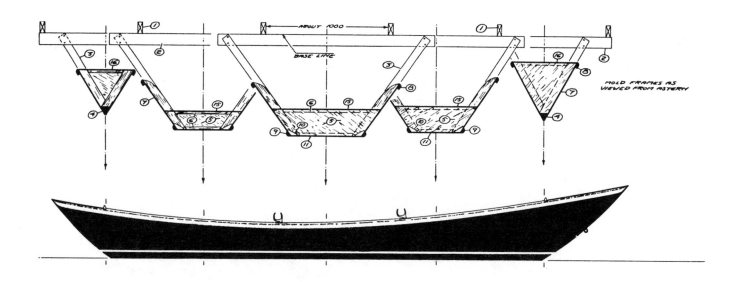

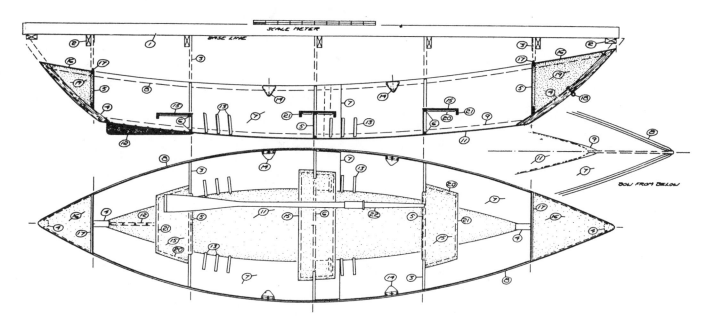

cessfully over the years, although their boats' shapes were dictated by considerations other than seaworthiness, such as nesting capability and economy.

Phil Bolger has designed several dories, and his Type V is a development of his Gloucester Light Dory. The main difference between the Type V and a typical dory is that the former has a pointed stern rather than the usual narrow "tombstone" transom. The purpose of the pointed stern is to simplify construction, and the boat is really quite easy to build using sheets of plywood.

The Type V is probably a trifle more stable than some, since she doesn't have an extremely narrow bot-

tom and has an exterior chine log, but she's still tippy. The designer thinks you'll be safe in all kinds of dirty weather however, provided you have sense enough not to stand up to admire the view. She certainly rows well and is dry, inexpensive, and handsome.

Of her forerunner design, Bolger wrote that when they stop him at the Pearly Gates and ask his excuse for entering, he'll tell them he designed the Gloucester Light Dory; and, he says, "They'll have to let me in."

Plans from Bolger Boats *by Philip C. Bolger, International Marine, 1983*

18

Harbinger

Length: 15 feet
Beam: 7 feet 1 inch
Sail Area: 151 square feet
Designer: Philip C. Bolger

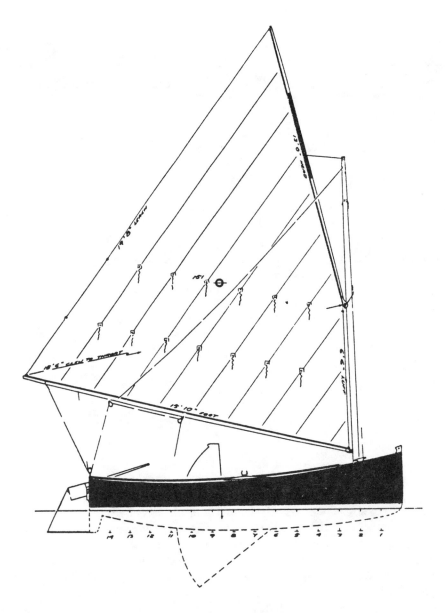

Two rather distinctive features set apart the Phil Bolger–designed *Harbinger* from the normal, daysailing, Cape Cod type of catboat. First, she is designed for rowing as well as sailing, and, second, she has well-rounded sections with a soft bilge. Another minor difference is her unusual skeg, which has a somewhat modern look.

The semicircular sections make *Harbinger* fairly tender initially, but she stiffens considerably when heeled. The shape of the sections reduces wetted sur-

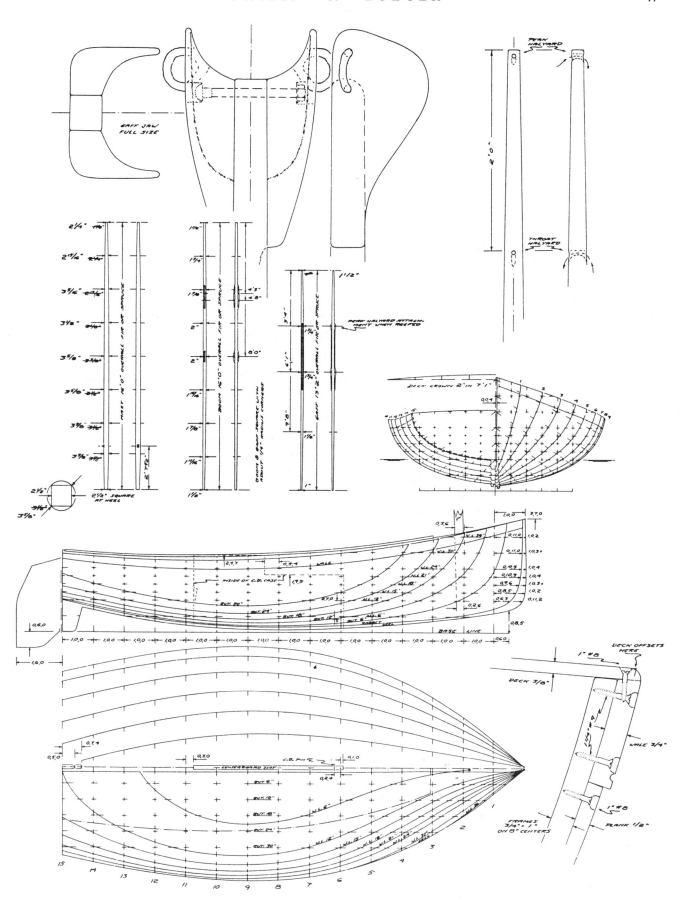

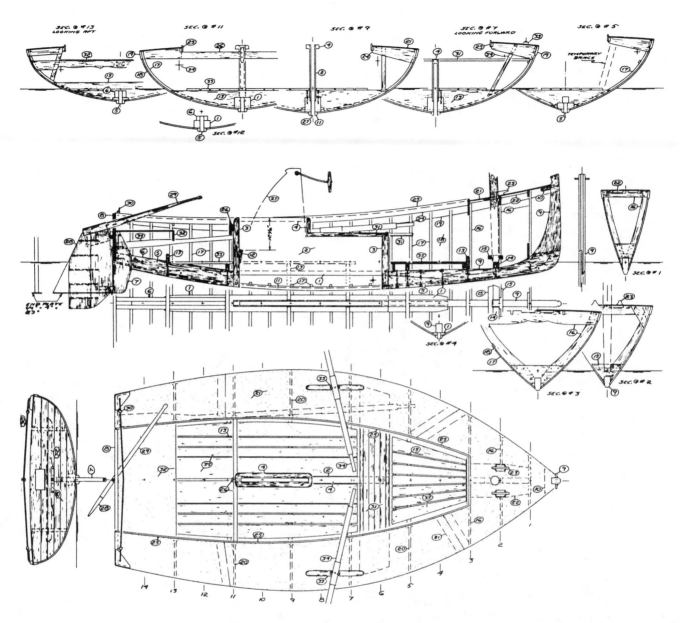

face, enabling easier propulsion under oars and sail. In fact, she can be moved with a modest rig, and this characteristic, along with generous flare and beam at the deck, gives her high resistance to capsizing. She is cedar planked and will float when swamped, but the designer recommends urethane-foam flotation.

To safeguard against shipping water, *Harbinger* has nice wide side decks, which are comfortable to sit on when hiking out in a breeze. You can also sit satisfactorily on the stern sheets, and there is a rowing thwart above the forward end of the centerboard trunk. I might like to have the oarlocks a bit farther outboard to keep the oars from scraping the deck edge, but Bolger, being such an experienced oarsman, has probably worked out the proper position.

The gaff mainsail is peaked up high, which is helpful when sailing close-hauled, but, according to the designer, somewhat compromises keeping consistent balance when reefed. Personally, I like to move a catboat's center of effort a little farther forward when reefed to alleviate the usual strong weather helm that heeling induces. I suspect that *Harbinger* will seldom need a deep reef because of her small rig and reserve stability at around 12 degrees of heel.

Plans from Bolger Boats *by Philip C. Bolger, International Marine, 1983*

19

Yarrow

Length on Deck: 16 feet 1 inch
Length on Waterline: 12 feet 11 inches
Beam: 5 feet
Draft: 2 feet 6 inches
Sail Area: 147 square feet
Designer: Philip C. Bolger

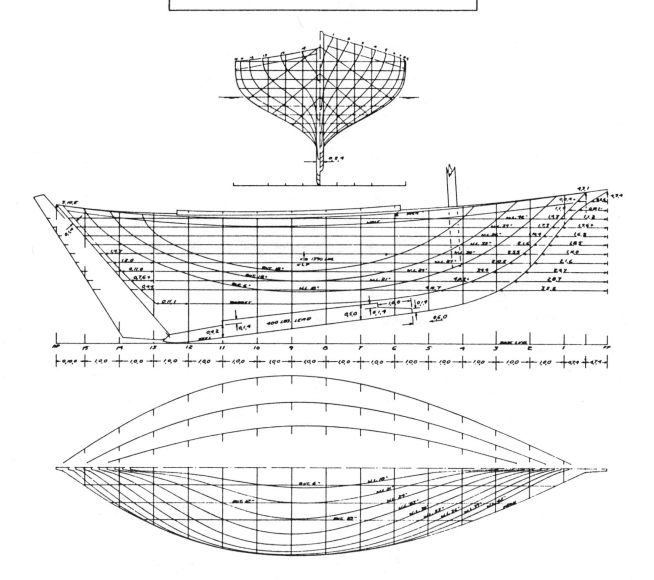

Among the loveliest hulls ever produced are the Tancook whalers, with their pointed sterns, sweeping sheer, wineglass sections, and balanced ends. This daysailing version, named *Yarrow,* designed by Phil Bolger, is particularly handsome, with her clipper bow and decorated trail boards.

Because of her deep body, fine stern, and short, effective sailing length, *Yarrow* is not extremely fast, and she may have a tendency to pitch at times, but she is a lively sailer — docile, forgiving, and a good chopcutter. The long keel with fairly deep drag should permit some self-steering capability, yet allow reasonable

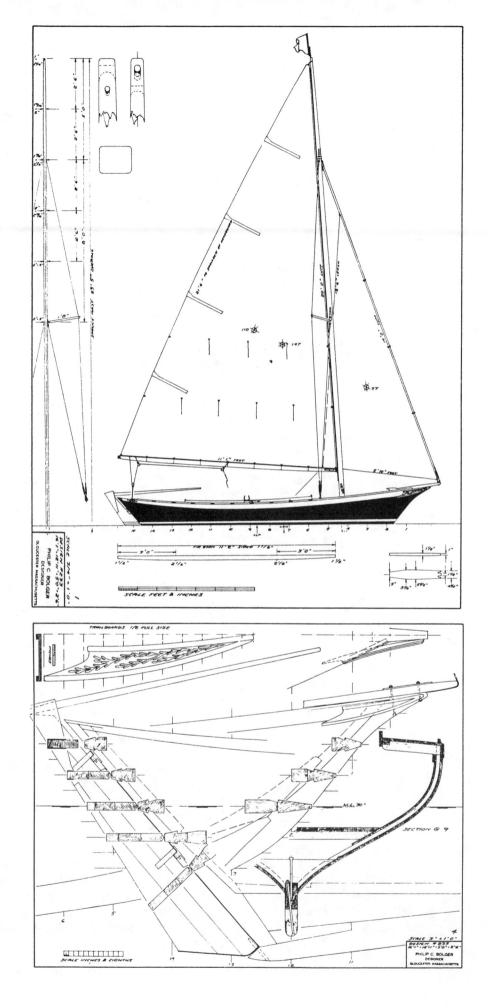

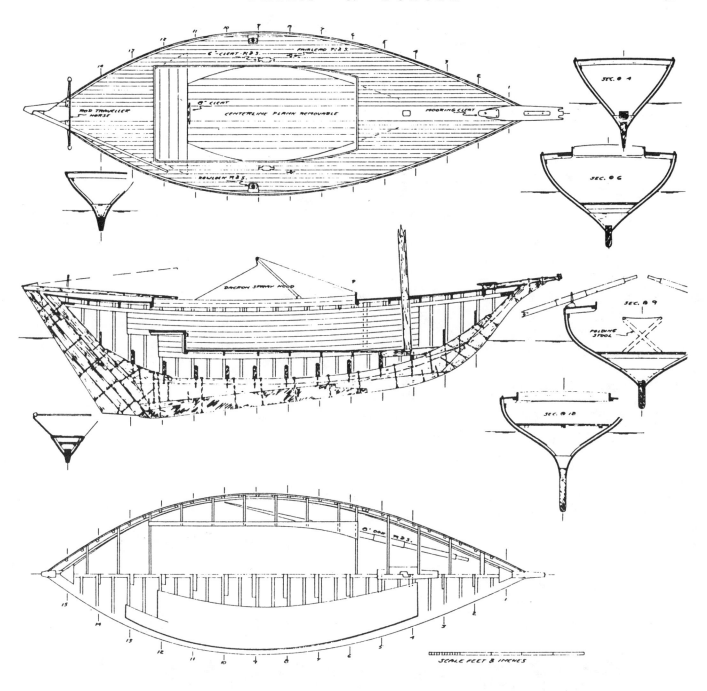

SCALE FEET & INCHES

maneuverability, while the tall rig and slack bilges suggest good ghosting ability. And you can make your own ash breeze, for she is fitted with oars and oarlocks.

The tall sloop rig is a handy one, as the small jib is easily managed, and the boat should keep reasonable balance and speed under main alone. The mast should have a fairly large section to prevent falloff at the head, but in a breeze with a shallow reef tied in, it would be very well supported by its low standing rigging. The bowsprit, although not long enough to need a bobstay, should be a stout one of oak or the equivalent.

Yarrow is built by conventional plank-on-frame construction. The deck, however, is somewhat unusual for a small boat in that it is glued strip planking, although it could be made of plywood.

Compared with the usual crop of stock fiberglass boats seen today, *Yarrow* stands out like a tern resting on the water between floating Clorox bottles.

Plans from Bolger Boats *by Philip C. Bolger, International Marine, 1983*

20

Dolphin

Length: 18 feet
Beam: 4 feet
Sail Area: 67 square feet
Designer: Philip C. Bolger

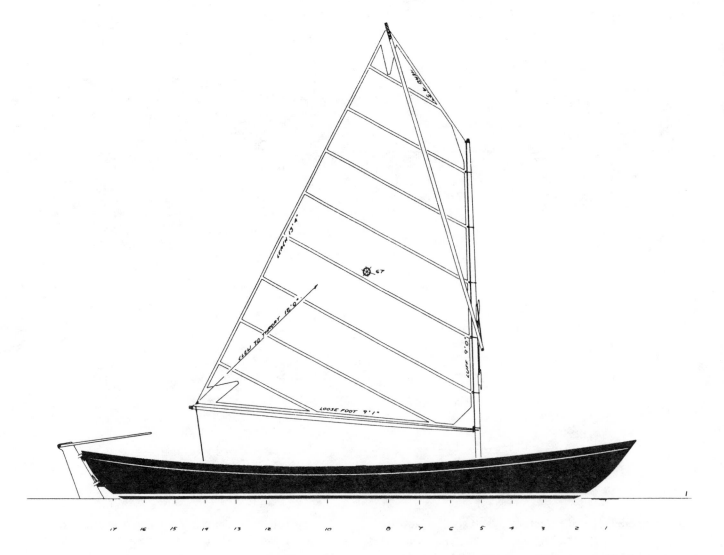

Whaleboats are certainly among the most graceful of double-enders and *Dolphin,* designed by Phil Bolger, is a particularly attractive one. She has shapely ends, a pretty sheer, a fine entrance for chop cutting, plenty of flare for dryness and reserve buoyancy, and nicely rounded sections that reduce wetted surface and provide a measure of seakindliness. Bolger says her midsection is similar to *Victoria* (design No. 16).

Although *Dolphin* is best propelled by oars, four of them at that, the designer has provided her with a small sail and centerboard. He is concerned about the resistance of the centerboard slot, but I think un-

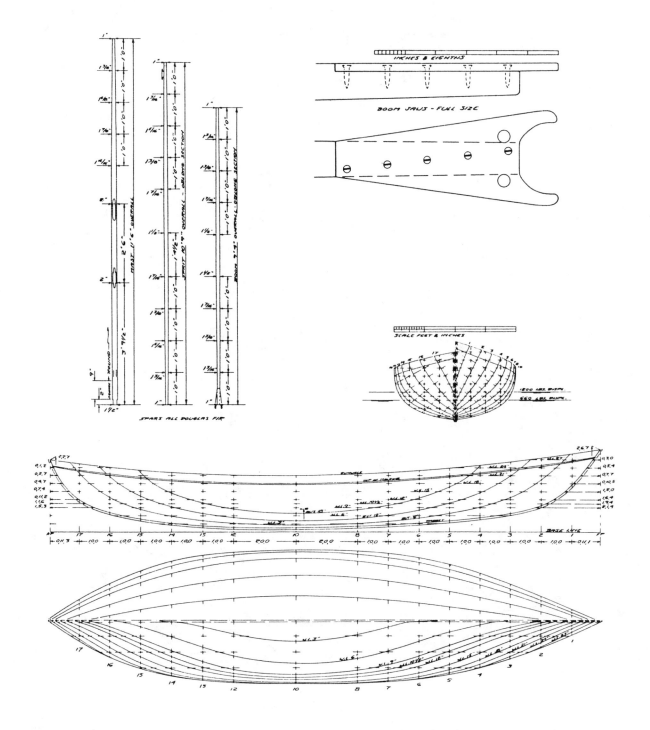

necessarily. Having rowed identical dinghies, one with and one without a daggerboard, I couldn't notice much difference in drag. Even if the whaleboat doesn't excel on all points of sailing, it is nice to have the sail in case you tire of rowing, and the small sprit rig is easy to set up and stow. *Dolphin* makes a good beach boat, with her shoal draft, ability to handle surf, and ease of trailering. Although she is fairly heavy, you could pull her out of water quite easily with a pair of air rollers. Her carvel construction is not inexpensive, but it's strong. Her beauty and practicality might, as Bolger suggests, "awaken the snobbery of the oarsman."

Plans from Bolger Boats *by Philip C. Bolger, International Marine, 1983*

· 21 ·

Black Skimmer

Length on Deck: 25 feet 3 inches
Beam: 7 feet
Sail Area: 304 square feet
Designer: Philip C. Bolger

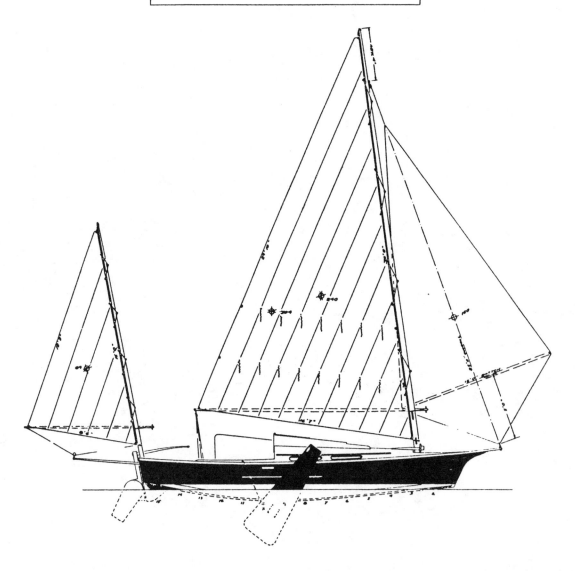

Aesthetically, the flat-bottomed sharpie is not everyone's cup of tea, but it is a classic sheltered-water type and has a number of advantages. "Commodore" Ralph Munroe even claimed the modified sharpie was suitable for offshore use, but I'd never recommend a boat with the short range of stability it has for long passages at sea. The main advantages of the sharpie are shallow draft, simplicity, and ease of construction, particularly with plywood.

Black Skimmer is a small version of several sharpies designed by Phil Bolger. She is not bad looking for her type, and her speed under sail might surprise some. Bolger says that he had four match races with one of his larger sharpie designs against a Pearson Triton, and

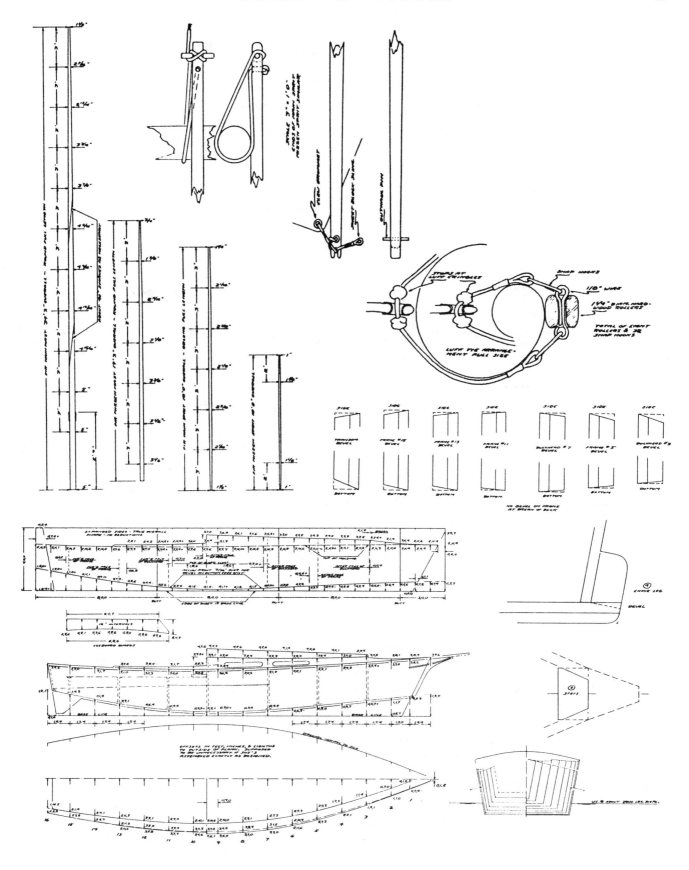

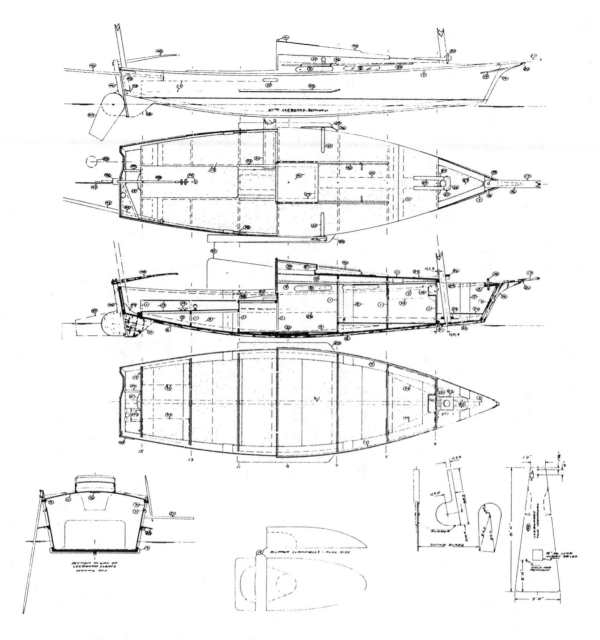

although he lost out when beating, he won all the races by virtue of his boat's running and reaching speed. Even though the sharpie had a much longer waterline length than the Triton, her performance impresses me, because I know how well a Triton can sail.

Black Skimmer's stayless rig is easy to handle, and she even has a hiking board that may be used to hold the boat down in a breeze when racing informally. The mizzen not only provides balance, but also helps prevent yawing when the boat is anchored. Despite some of the disadvantages of leeboards, they are valuable on this type of boat to allow more room below. Guards hold them out at an efficient angle to minimize leeway.

Although there is not much in the way of accommodations, there seems to be sufficient sitting headroom as well as room for a couple of low bunks and a simple galley. The designer said he has lived in her for as long as a month. With her kick-up rudder and very shoal draft, you could always find plenty of swinging room in any anchorage.

Plans from Bolger Boats *by Philip C. Bolger, International Marine, 1983*

· 22 ·

Burgundy

Length on Deck: 28 feet
Beam: 6 feet 3 inches
Draft: 3 feet 8 inches
Displacement: 3,500 pounds
Sail Area: 271 square feet
Designer: Philip C. Bolger

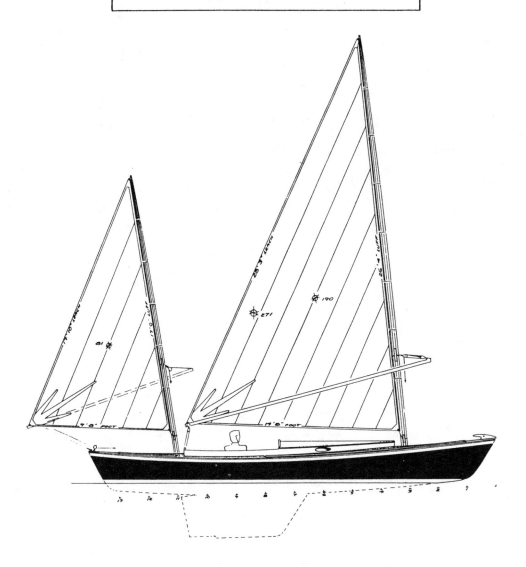

The cat-ketch *Burgundy,* designed by Phil Bolger, is a flat-bottomed boat with a fin keel. The benefit of shoal draft is lost with the keel, but still the flat-bottomed-hull form simplifies building, and the fin has certain advantages. It enhances windward performance, enables the attachment of deep ballast (1,270 pounds of lead) to help prevent capsizing, and avoids the need to handle a centerboard or leeboards. It also obviates the problems of a leaking and space-robbing centerboard trunk and of leeboards collecting flotsam. Because of her external

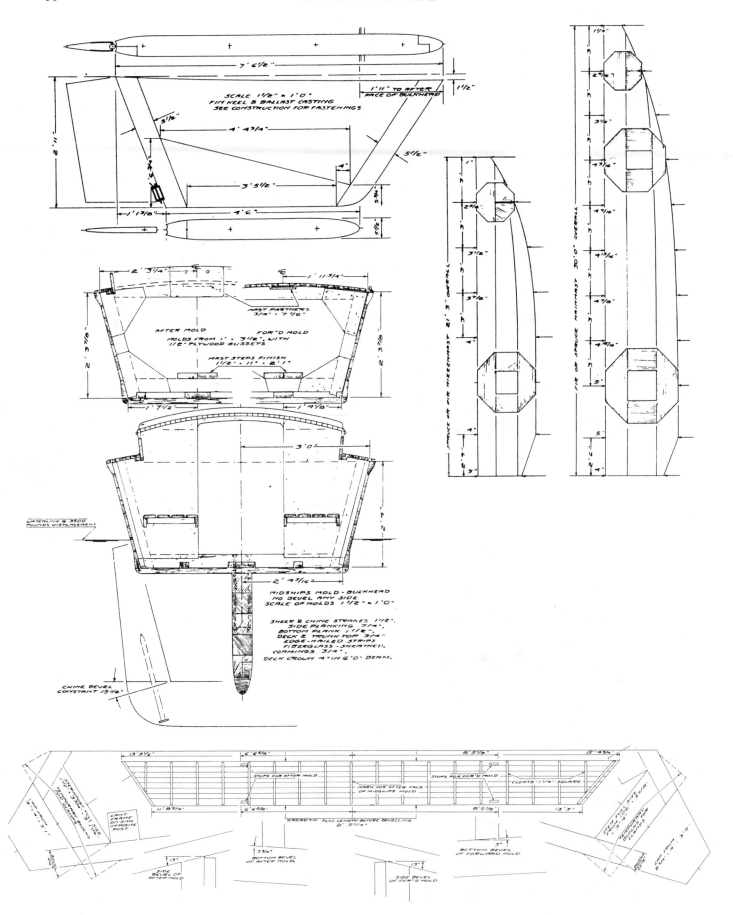

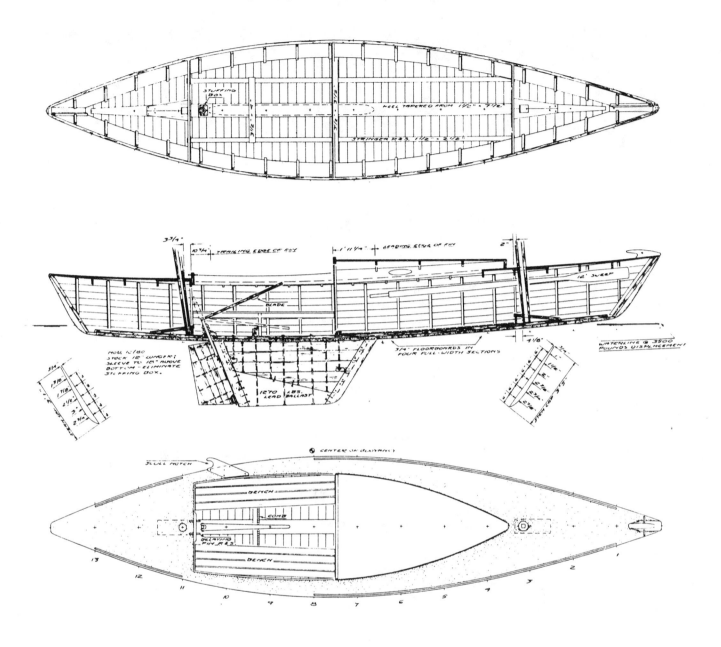

ballast, which is about 36 percent of her displacement, *Burgundy* can be quite narrow to allow high reserve stability yet easy initial heeling to prevent pounding.

The cat-ketch rig with sprit booms is effective and easy to handle and balance. One advantage of having the sail area's center quite far aft is that it allows a short fin (for low wetted surface) far aft where it can accept a keel-attached rudder. This positioning of the rudder provides proper tiller placement, a flap effect for keel lift, and negligible rudder ventilation. Were the rudder farther forward, it would provide poor steering control.

Auxiliary power is supplied with a 12-foot sweep that is operated from the port-side sculling notch. There is not much room below, but I'm glad the designer resisted the temptation to add a higher cabin trunk, because that would have spoiled the looks of a handsome boat.

Plans from 30-Odd Boats *by Philip C. Bolger, International Marine, 1982*

EDWARD BREWER

23

Cape Cod Cat

Length on Deck: 21 feet 7 inches
Beam: 10 feet
Displacement: 5,850 pounds
Sail Area: 374 square feet
Designer: Edward S. Brewer

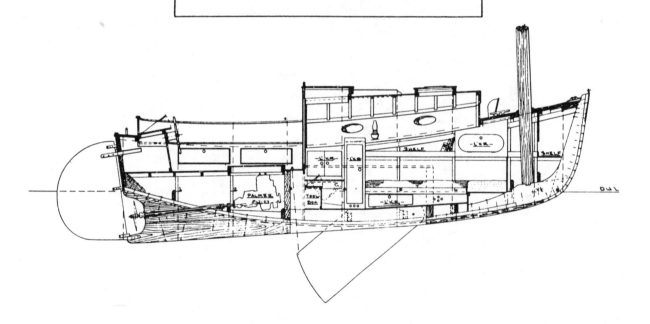

Although largely self-taught, Edward S. ''Ted'' Brewer is one of America's most gifted and versatile yacht designers. His work usually displays a unique amalgamation of what is best in both traditional and modern design. He is also an astute critic and commentator on design and construction.

Ted says his 22-foot Cape Cod catboat is probably his most popular design. He has sold over 300 sets of plans to people as far away as Europe, Africa, South America, New Zealand, and Australia. Her popularity is due not only to her ease of handling, good looks, and practicality, but also to her hard-chine hull form, which allows easy construction with marine plywood.

Ten feet of beam gives this boat great initial stability and, of course, unusual room in the cockpit and cabin. Accommodations are comfortable for two, and there is even a degree of privacy with the semienclosed head. Two nice features are the wood-burning stove, which adds to the cabin's coziness, and the cockpit icebox, which puts cold beer at the working crew's fingertips yet is reachable from the galley. The plans call for a two-cylinder Palmer engine under the cockpit sole.

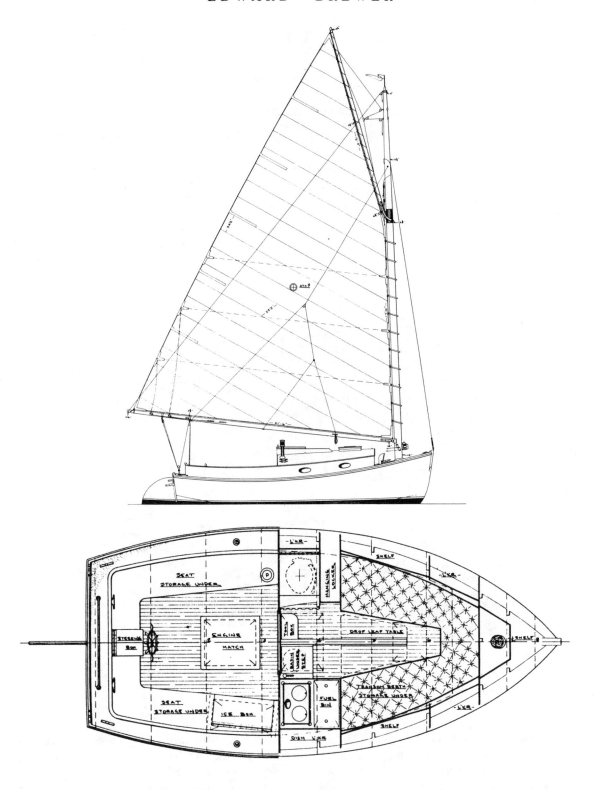

A minor variation from the norm for this type of cat is a slightly overhanging bow. This feature provides a better stay angle and a bit more room on the foredeck, while simplifying construction. A steering wheel eases steering and allows more cockpit room.

Knowing Ted Brewer's considerable experience as a sailor, I'll bet this cat sails well for a boat of her size and type.

Plans from Understanding Boat Design *by Edward S. Brewer and Jim Betts, International Marine, 1980*

24

Chappaquiddick

Length on Deck: 25 feet
Beam: 12 feet 6 inches
Draft: 3 feet 1 inch
Sail Area: 522 square feet
Designer: Edward S. Brewer

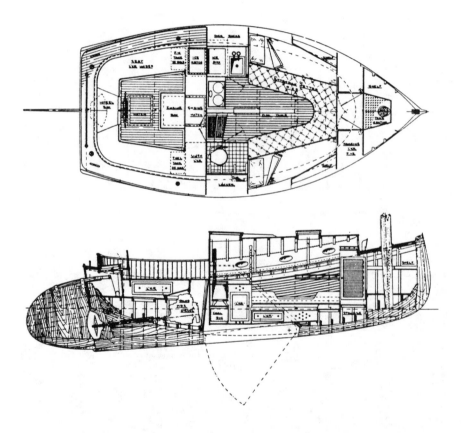

Another catboat designed by Ted Brewer is the 25-foot *Chappaquiddick*. Many of the remarks made about the 22-foot Brewer Cape Cod cat (design No. 23) apply to this boat, except that she is larger and proportionately more spacious. The extra size allows a completely enclosed head, a large galley with sink, and extension settees under pilot berths. There is also plenty of room for stowage and lockers up forward.

The *Chappaquiddick* has a more authentic appearance than the smaller Brewer cat. She looks a lot like many of the old-time Cape Cod cats, with her bold sheer and bulldoglike, retroussé stem. These features give her a lot of character, or at least nostalgic appeal.

The sail is easy to handle and efficient with its peaked-up gaff and lazyjacks. Ted Brewer wrote me that one enthusiastic owner told him how he sailed into

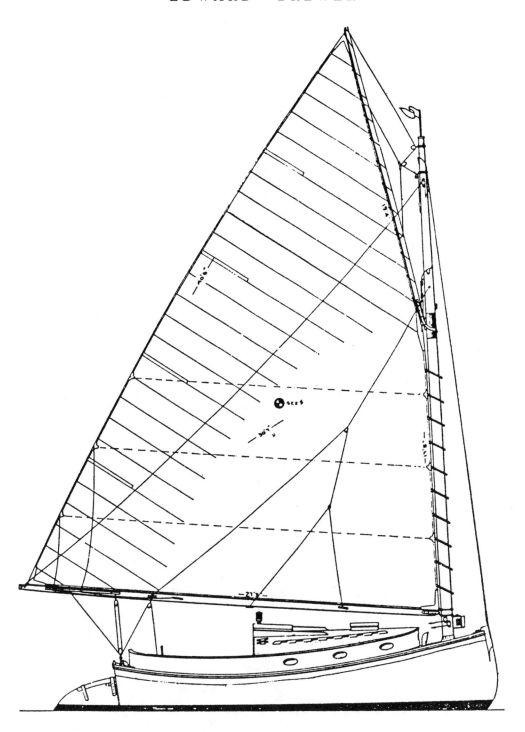

Newport, Rhode Island, in a blow with his boat reefed down, heeling only a little, and was able to keep up with racing yachts that were knocked down and making heavy weather of it.

The *Chappaquiddick* was first built of wood in Taiwan in 1970, but later fiberglass models were available from One Design Marine, Inc. The designer writes that he has also made the boat available in a double-chine hull, minus the retroussé bow, for plywood construction.

Plans from The Catboat Book, *edited by John M. Leavens, International Marine, 1973*

25

Jason

Length on Deck: 34 feet 6 inches
Length on Waterline: 27 feet 4 inches
Beam: 11 feet 2 inches
Draft: 5 feet
Displacement: 16,800 pounds
Sail Area: 634 square feet
Designer: Edward S. Brewer

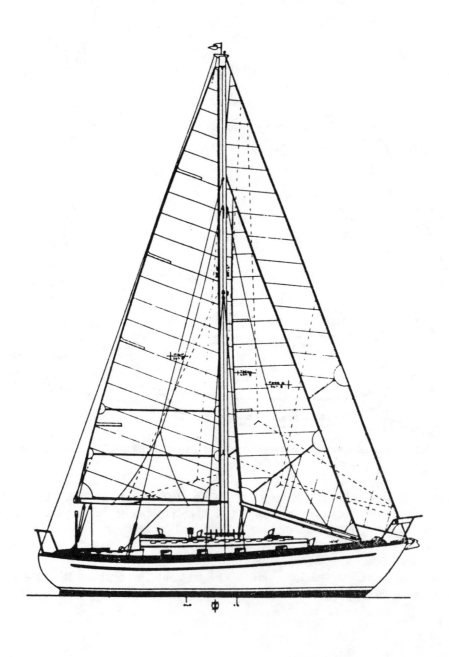

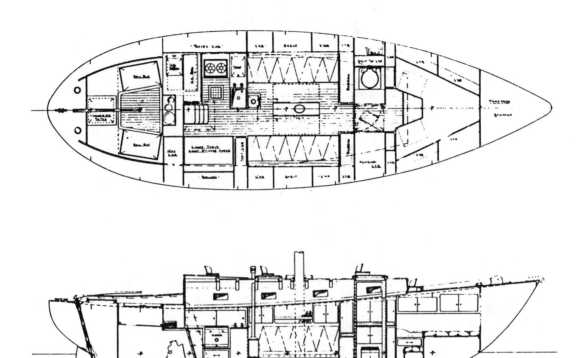

Seagoing double-enders often have a major fault: they can be sluggish sailers in light to moderate winds. Not so the Jason 35, designed by Ted Brewer. I know she is fast from firsthand experience, because I've sailed alongside her in my Ohlson 38, which does well in any company. Although moderately heavy with a fairly large wetted-surface area for seakindliness and steadiness, *Jason* has a tall rig and plenty of sail area to drive her in all conditions, while her lines forward are sufficiently fine for good performance in head seas. The lateral-plane cutout abaft the keel helps reduce the wetted surface and affords maneuverability with little sacrifice to directional stability.

She has excellent accommodations with plenty of privacy and ventilation and such desirable features as a large chart desk, a U-shaped galley, and a heating stove. Her cutter rig, with self-tending staysail and main-boom

gallows, is ideal for shorthanded offshore work. The small cockpit well and bridge deck are good seagoing features.

Designed as a custom job for a specific client, the *Jason* attracted enough attention to cause a small demand. Hulls are built of fiberglass by the Seeman C-Flex method, which is one-off construction within the capability of a good amateur builder. Bare hulls can be obtained for owner completion. *Tellina,* the Jason 35 I sailed alongside, was completed by owner Robert Franks, who turned out a beautifully finished boat with several interesting modifications to the original belowdecks plan.

Plans from Understanding Boat Design *by Edward S. Brewer and Jim Betts, International Marine, 1980*

26

Pinky Sloop

Length on Deck: 34 feet 5 inches
Length on Waterline: 30 feet 4 inches
Beam: 11 feet 4 inches
Draft: 5 feet
Displacement: 23,900 pounds
Sail Area: 742 square feet
Designer: Edward S. Brewer

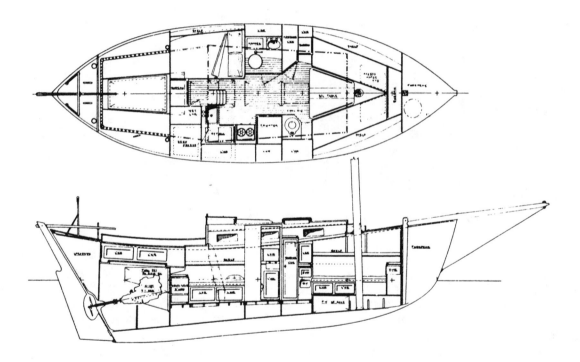

Pinkies were early New England sharp-stern fishing boats noted for their seaworthiness and comfort in heavy weather. An exceptionally pretty boat with its sweeping sheer and double-ended hull form, the pinky was an irresistable attraction for George M. Moffett. He wanted one similar to, but larger than, a contemporary pinky model known as the Quoddy Pilot, and he wanted her made of fiberglass for less upkeep. Thus, he commissioned Ted Brewer to design him a 34-footer for one-off construction.

This boat, named *Sunshine,* was given somewhat somewhat unusual accommodations with a double quarter berth, bureau and wet locker abaft the companionway ladder, and saloon forward. Several appealing features are the splendid galley, large enclosed head, and coal stove. There is even a small forepeak.

Sunshine is heavy and has relatively small sail area for ease of handling, but she is quite fast and stable in a breeze and requires little effort to handle, with her self-tending jib, lazyjacks, and gallows frame. I would rig a

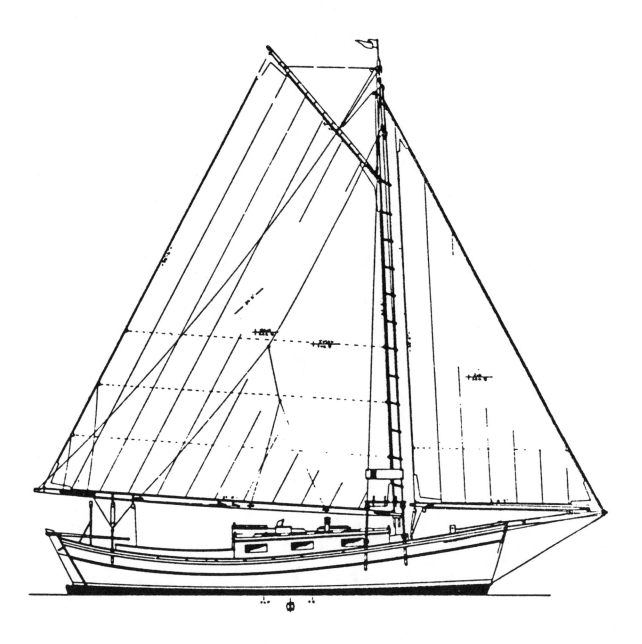

downhaul on the jib to minimize any need to venture out on the bowsprit.

Early pinkies were very fine aft and were usually given pink-type false sterns, which helped keep their sterns dry, but Ted Brewer's design is probably fuller in the quarters and no doubt has more buoyancy and volume aft to accommodate an engine under the cockpit.

George Moffett is now deceased, but Ted Brewer tells me he has heard that *Sunshine* is still sailed by his wife. Undoubtedly, this handsome craft attracts attention wherever she goes.

Plans from Understanding Boat Design *by Edward S. Brewer and Jim Betts, International Marine, 1980*

27

Brewer 39

Length on Deck: 39 feet 6 inches
Length on Waterline: 32 feet 4 inches
Beam: 11 feet 11 inches
Draft: 5 feet 10 inches
Displacement: 18,250 pounds
Sail Area: 721 square feet
Designer: Edward S. Brewer

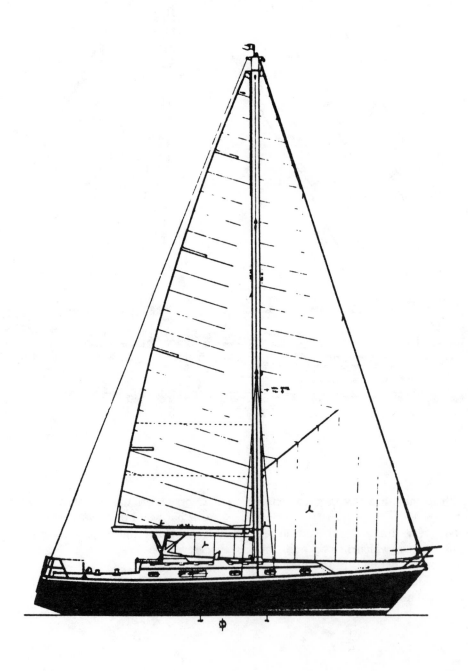

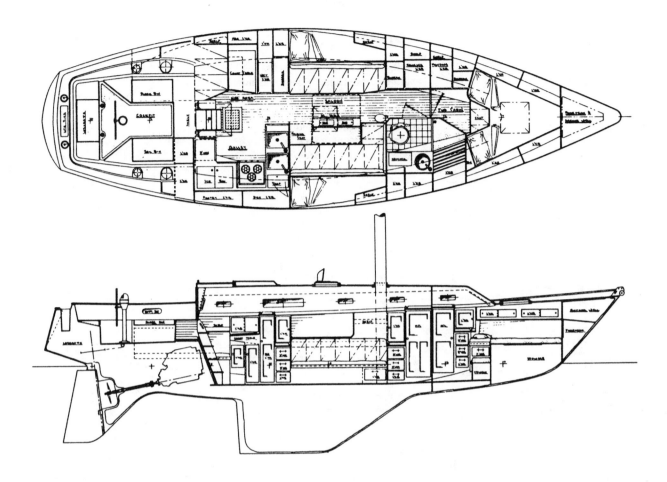

When a designer allows one of his stock boats to be named after him, you can be reasonably sure that he likes the design. And why wouldn't Ted Brewer be pleased with the Brewer 39? She is an attractive-looking, modern racing-cruiser with a high degree of versatility, being a fast boat yet comfortable enough for extensive cruising. She is also an able boat and not extreme in any way.

The accommodations are spacious with 6½-foot berths, a huge U-shaped galley, stall shower, chart table, and ample storage space. An interesting and somewhat unusual feature is the Y-shaped cockpit, which gives the helmsman room to pass by and stand on either side of the wheel, but keeps the well reasonably small for seaworthiness.

The Brewer 39 appears to have good windward ability with her high-aspect-ratio rig and reasonably deep, moderate-area fin keel, which has a high-lift NACA (National Advisory Commission for Aeronautics) sectional shape. The large masthead foretriangle gives her plenty of power, and she can carry her sail well with her generous beam and 40 percent ballast-to-displacement ratio. The sizable skeg provides good rudder support and directional stability. She should have much better manners than the more extreme grand-prix-type racers.

Highly suitable for family cruising, the Brewer 39 also has considerable racing potential under the Performance Handicap Racing Fleet (PHRF) and Measurement Handicap System (MHS) rules. She is built of laminated mahogany with a cored fiberglass deck and trunk by Berwick Yachts of Berwick, Ontario, Canada, and is available in all forms of completion.

Plans from Understanding Boat Design *by Edward S. Brewer and Jim Betts, International Marine, 1980*

· 28 ·

Black Velvet II

Length on Deck: 43 feet 2 inches
Length on Waterline: 35 feet 4 inches
Beam: 12 feet 9 inches
Draft: 6 feet 4 inches
Displacement: 24,800 pounds
Sail Area: 895 square feet
Designer: Edward S. Brewer

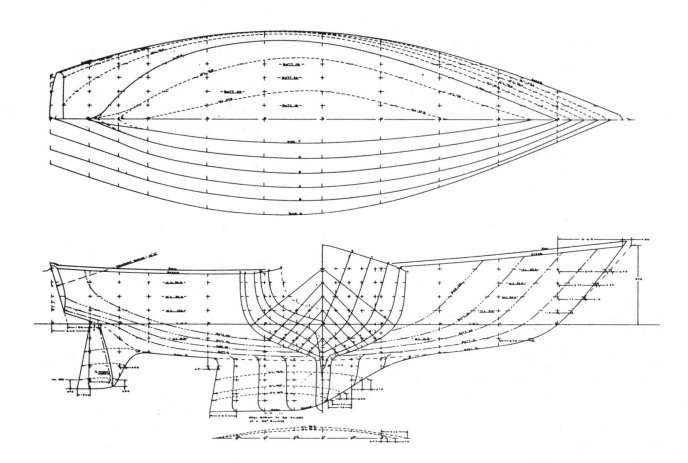

You can tell that Ted Brewer especially likes his *Black Velvet II* design, because he has her reduced profile plan on his letterhead. She is a forerunner design to Ted's Whitby 42, which in recent years has been in great demand. I wrote up the Whitby 42 in the book *Choice*

Yacht Designs, and she is one of my favorite cruisers. In some respects, though, I like *Black Velvet II* even better. She has a bit less freeboard and a more cutaway underbody for less wetted surface area. She also has a more efficient keel with deeper draft for better windward per-

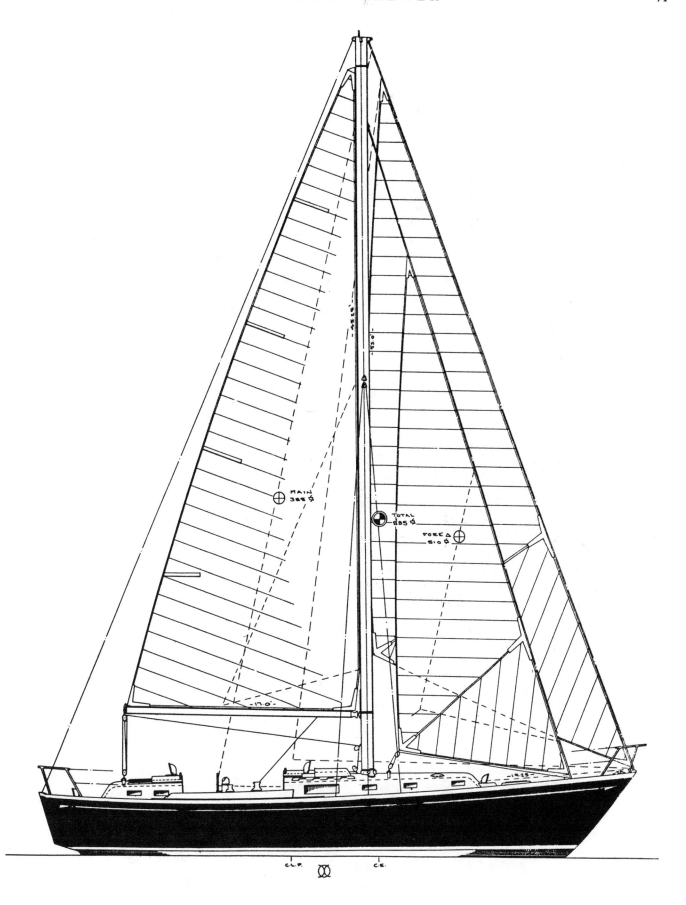

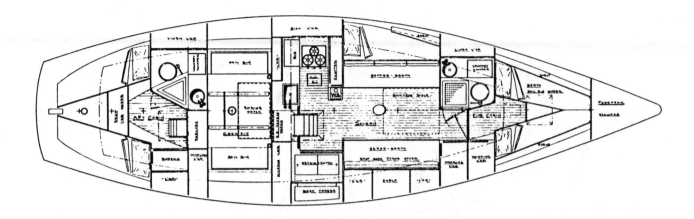

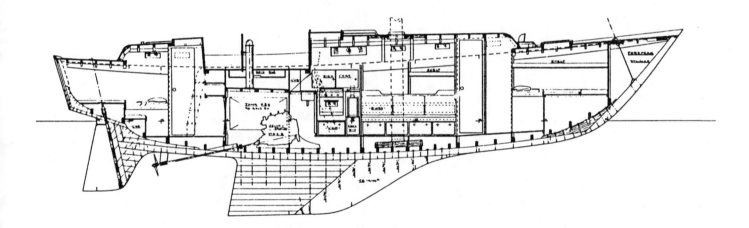

formance. The trade-off, of course, is that *Black Velvet II* is not a gunkholer, but she is, in my opinion, a somewhat better sea boat with a greater range of stability. She should also be more maneuverable, although perhaps at a slight cost in course keeping.

Black Velvet II is about the last work in accommodations comfort and privacy for two or three couples. The center cockpit completely separates the staterooms, and there is an enclosed head for each. About the only feature that the boat doesn't have is a chart desk, but charts can be spread out quite satisfactorily on top of the refrigerator.

The cutter rig with self-tending staysail is easy to handle yet weatherly and fast, with a large masthead jib. To give some idea of the boat's speed, the Cape North version of the design won first overall in the PHRF division of the 1983 Swiftsure Race.

Construction is of strip-planked mahogany on bulkhead framing, but the model that Cape North of Hong Kong produced is made of fiberglass. Ted's former partner, Bob Wallstrom, did the fiberglass construction plans for the Cape North 43.

Plans from Sea Sense *by Richard Henderson, International Marine, 1979*

29

Kingsland 45

Length on Deck: 45 feet 3 inches
Length on Waterline: 36 feet 8 inches
Beam: 14 feet
Draft: 6 feet
Displacement: 40,000 pounds
Sail Area: 1,159 square feet
Designer: Edward S. Brewer

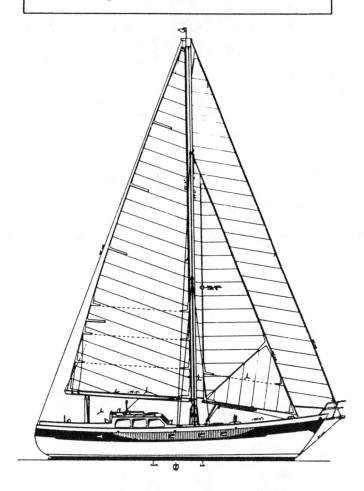

The Kingsland 45 seems to be an enlarged version of the Jason 35 (design No. 25), modified for steel construction and with a pilothouse. She is a sturdy boat of heavy displacement with large tank capacity suitable for a small family to cruise the world or live aboard. The layout below allows plenty of sleeping areas, comfortable seating, a large shower stall, navigation area, and even a spacious workshop, which could be converted to a sleeping area with two more bunks if so desired.

Although her freeboard may seem a bit high, it may be reduced optically by painting a wide stripe as shown in the sailplan. The cockpit is over 10 feet long, but has a small well with large drains for safety in the event that she should happen to "ship it green." There are plenty of hatches, windows, and Dorade vents for good light and ventilation.

The rig is a tall one, but with the self-tending staysail, a roller-furling jib, and an efficient jiffy reefing system for the mainsail, the boat should not be difficult to handle. She is undoubtedly stiff with her broad beam,

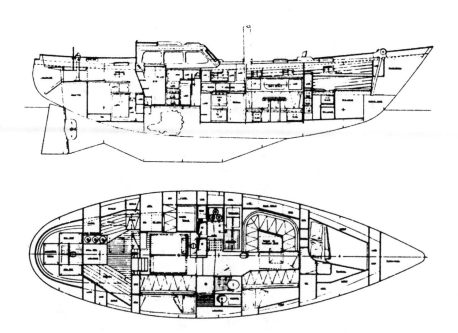

heavy displacement, ample ballast, and deep tanks. Running backstays would be a worthwhile addition for heavy-weather safety and to tighten the forestay for windward work.

The hull is a radiused-bilge form that closely resembles the round-bilge hull but simplifies construc-

tion. Indeed, the first two Kingslands were built by amateurs.

Plans from Understanding Boat Design *by Edward S. Brewer and Jim Betts, International Marine, 1980*

· 30 ·

Sophia Christina

Length on Deck: 46 feet 1 inch
Length on Waterline: 40 feet
Beam: 13 feet 5 inches
Draft: 6 feet 7 inches
Displacement: 48,000 pounds
Sail Area: 1,354 square feet (four lowers)
Designer: Edward S. Brewer

The marine historian Howard Chapelle has written that *Lillie* (of the late 1800s) "was considered the handsomest of the Boston pilot schooners in her time." Ted Brewer styled *Sophia Christina* after *Lillie,* so it is little

wonder that she is appealing to the eye. Chapelle also wrote, "Taking all types of commercial schooners into consideration, the pilot boat most closely resembles the yacht in her requirements, since she carries no cargo and

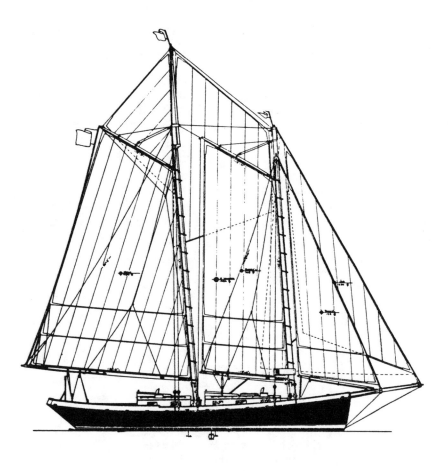

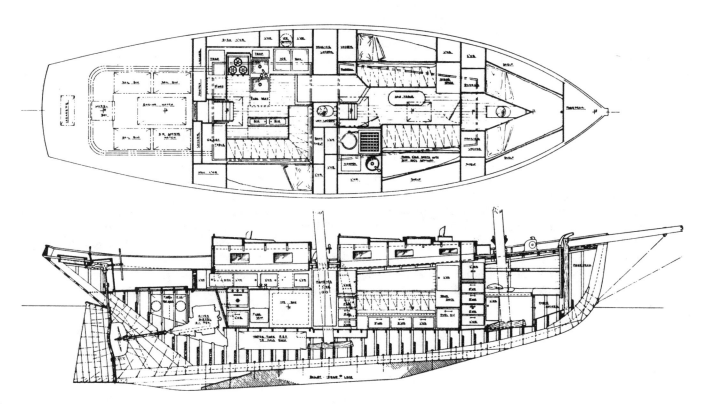

has to be fast and seaworthy.'' He further said that pilots attached great importance to easy motion. *Sophia Christina* has all of these qualities.

Of her speed, Ted Brewer recently wrote that she won the schooner race at the 1983 Wooden Boat Festival in Port Townsend, Washington, beating many larger marconi-rigged craft boat-for-boat. He says she is surprisingly fast.

With her two cabin trunks and separate companionways, *Sophia Christina* offers a lot of privacy, and her accommodations have proven ideal for charter parties. Berths are 6 feet 7 inches long and are fitted into three separate cabins. There is ample room for stowage and plenty of deck space. She recently passed U.S. Coast Guard requirements for 30 day-passengers.

Built of wood by Freya Boat Works in Anacortes, Washington, *Sophia Christina* is carvel planked on steam-bent frames. A sister is now being built in France by a yard that specializes in workboat replicas and traditional yachts.

Ted Brewer sums her up with three words: ''A real honey.''

Plans from Understanding Boat Design *by Edward S. Brewer and Jim Betts, International Marine, 1980*

· 31 ·

Blue Jeans

Length on Deck: 46 feet 8 inches
Length on Waterline: 32 feet 8 inches
Beam: 13 feet 6 inches
Draft: 5 feet
Displacement: 28,500 pounds
Sail Area: 966 square feet
Designer: Edward S. Brewer

An attractive boat for extensive cruising and fast passages is the Brewer-designed cutter *Blue Jeans*. She has a flush deck that provides lots of room below, adds to the boat's strength, and allows plenty of deck space. The accommodations are spacious and private, although the owner's stateroom is located where there will be a fair amount of motion when the seas are kicking up. A nice feature is the fo'c's'le with workbench and sail locker. I doubt if you could get a large sail bag through the forward hatch, but you could get it through the hatch in the owner's cabin.

The rig does not require much work for a small crew, since the mainsail has an area of only 390 square feet and the staysail is self-tending. *Blue Jeans* should be able to make good progress to windward with her centerboard down. The moderately shoal keel is deep enough to allow low placement of ballast for adequate stability, while permitting reasonable performance to windward without the board; yet the draft is not too deep for a shallow harbor.

The hull is built of Airex-cored fiberglass, but plans for steel construction are also available. Regardless of the hull material, the plans call for teak decks.

Blue Jeans has a particularly attractive stern in my opinion. She is a bit high sided but should look just right when her ample tanks are filled and she is loaded down for a voyage to distant places.

Plans from Understanding Boat Design *by Edward S. Brewer and Jim Betts, International Marine, 1980*

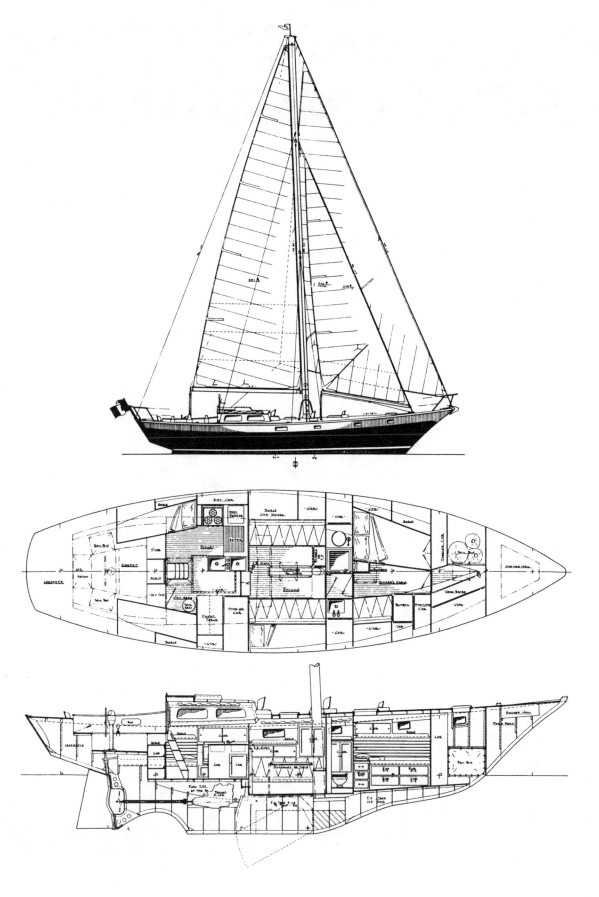

SAMUEL S. CROCKER, JR.

32

Dog Watch

Length on Deck: 16 feet
Length on Waterline: 15 feet 6 inches
Beam: 7 feet 6 inches
Draft: 1 foot 9 inches
Sail Area: 211 square feet
Designer: Samuel S. Crocker, Jr.

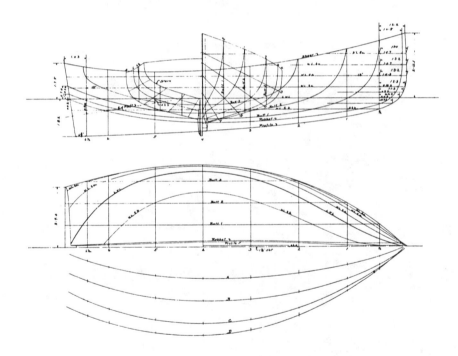

The designer of *Dog Watch* is Samuel S. Crocker, Jr., the veteran naval architect who was the first of many associates in the famous John G. Alden firm. For Alden's firm and later on his own, Crocker designed a number of catboats, and *Dog Watch* is a fine example of the type.

Despite her canine name and her sloop rig, this boat looks like a catboat all right and a much larger one than she actually is. Her catlike characteristics are the broad beam, huge cockpit, shoal draft, plumb stem, fine entrance, wide transom, low deadrise, and bold sheer. Such a design gives her high initial stability, plenty of room for daysailing, and an ability to gunkhole, as well as a look of authenticity.

Most catboats don't carry jibs, but I like the idea. The boat would handle well under main alone, of course, but the jib gives extra speed in light weather. There are also certain times when reaching that a cat has a strong

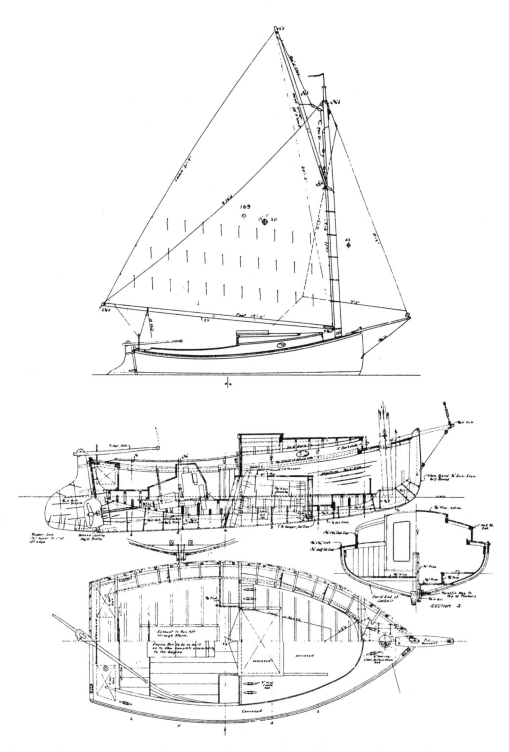

weather helm and the jib will relieve it. To simplify handling sail on the tiny foredeck, the jib is roller furling.

The cabin is amazingly roomy for a 16-footer, and the two bunks are 6 feet 3 inches long. Although engines in the cockpit can take up valuable space, there's plenty of room for the iron jib in this boat, and its box makes a good foot brace when the boat is heeling. Despite her tiny size, *Dog Watch* is a real cruising catboat.

Plans from The Fourth Book of Good Boats *by Roger C. Taylor, International Marine 1984*

33

Brownie

Length on Deck: 31 feet 11 inches
Length on Waterline: 23 feet 6 inches
Beam: 8 feet 6 inches
Draft: 5 feet 6 inches
Displacement: 5½ tons
Sail Area: 590 square feet
Designer: Samuel S. Crocker, Jr.

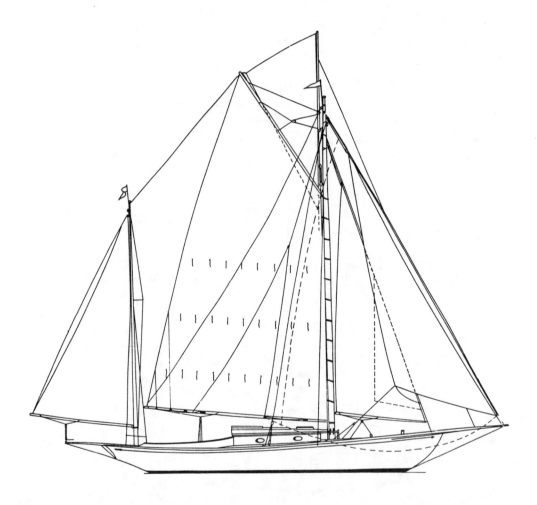

Roger Taylor of International Marine, publisher of this book, is a lucky fellow to have spent his youth with such a lovely little yawl as *Brownie*. A prize possession of his father, *Brownie* was one of the very best designs of many good ones that Sam Crocker produced. Roger wrote all about the yawl, waxing poetic about a few memorable sails aboard her, in his book *Good Boats*.

She's a smart sailer and especially fast beating to windward, even with her gaff main. The Taylors effectively used a gaff vang led to the mizzenmast's head to reduce sail twist. About her only fault, said Roger, was a quick roll at times caused by her deep, heavy keel ballast. Perhaps this could be alleviated by giving her a taller marconi mainmast. Whether gaff or jibheaded,

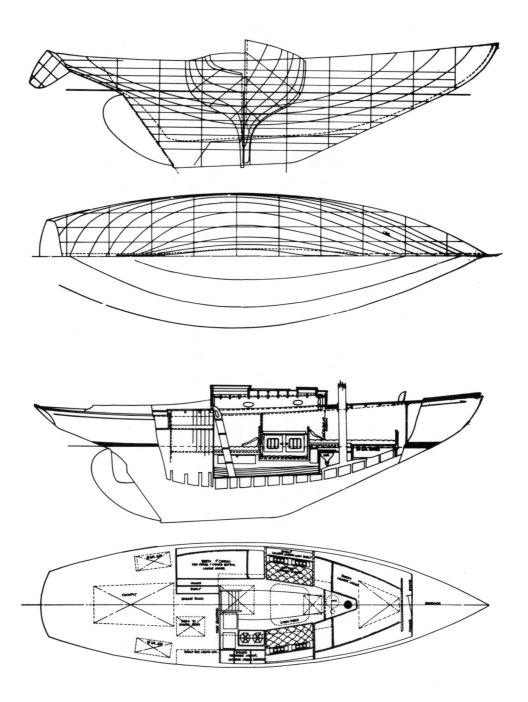

though, the rig is versatile, offering a variety of sail combinations for any kind of weather.

The arrangement below does not crowd in more bunks than are really needed, and it is refreshing to see seats that are intended just for seats on such a small cruiser. Roger complained about the head arrangement, however, and said a better plan would have been a bucket in the engine room. A modern builder might want to trade off some engine-room space for a small enclosed head.

Nowadays, you seldom see boats as beautiful as *Brownie.*

Plans from Good Boats *by Roger C. Taylor, International Marine, 1977*

34

Aunt Sara

Length on Deck: 35 feet
Length on Waterline: 28 feet 7 inches
Beam: 10 feet 10 inches
Draft: 4 feet
Sail Area: 700 square feet
Designer: Samuel S. Crocker, Jr.

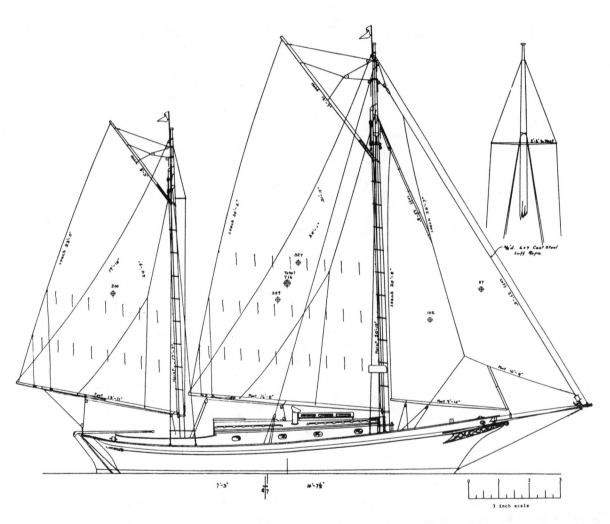

Occasionally, I used to sail and even race aboard a clipper-bowed yawl named *Milky Way* designed by Sam Crocker that was quite similar in size and looks to his *Aunt Sara*. *Milky Way* impressed me as an exceedingly handsome, able, steady, and comfortable boat that was surprisingly fast. The same could be said of *Aunt Sara*, although she has 2 feet less draft than *Milky Way* and a gaff rig, rather than marconi. She could not possibly sail as well to windward as *Milky Way*, but she should be just about as fast on other points of sailing and obviously is more suitable for shallow-water cruising. *Aunt Sara*'s outboard rudder is all the way aft for effec-

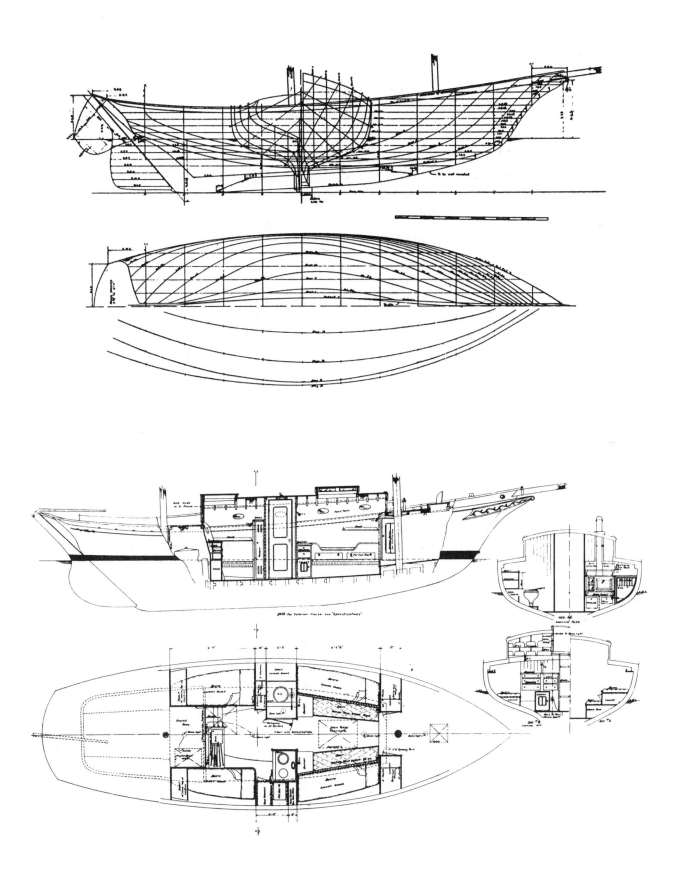

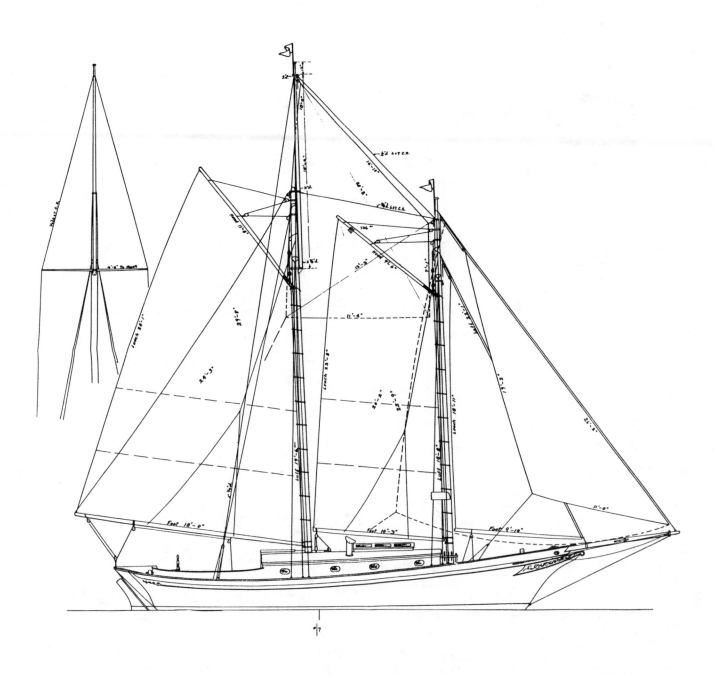

tive steering, and it has a rather modern shape for a boat that was built in 1929. The propeller aperture would cause less drag if it were smaller.

There is a choice of rigs for *Aunt Sara*. Although the ketch version would be slightly easier to handle, I might choose the schooner because it possesses such character, is able to get more sail aloft in light airs, and sacrifices very little if any in the size of the foretriangle. Also, I think I'd rather have the after mast planted in the after cabin, rather than in the middle of the cockpit.

The below-decks arrangement is practical and comfortable for a crew of four, but I'd like to move the starboard quarter berth farther aft where it does not intrude into the splendid galley.

I sometimes wonder why there are not more sensible and handsome cruising boats like *Aunt Sara* being built today.

Plans from The Fourth Book of Good Boats *by Roger C. Taylor, International Marine, 1984*

WILLIAM GARDEN

35

Eel

Length on Deck: 18 feet 6 inches
Length on Waterline: 14 feet 10 inches
Beam: 6 feet
Draft: 10 inches
Displacement: 1,000 pounds
Sail Area: 201 square feet
Designer: William Garden

This boat is well named, because she looks slippery, and with her draft of less than a foot, she could snake her way up the shallowest eel rut. She was inspired by a canoe yawl of the same name that George Holmes designed and Uffa Fox publicized in one of his books on yacht design, *Sailing, Seamanship, and Yacht Construction.*

The *Eel* presented here was designed by the highly respected, extremely versatile naval architect William Garden, who has been practicing for decades in the Seattle–Victoria, B.C., region of the Pacific Northwest. Of this designer, offshore powerboat authority Robert Beebe has written, "From dinghies to 110-foot luxury yachts, he has done everything, and done it with a style so distinctive that one is in no doubt, when one sees an example of his work, that it *is* a Garden design."

Garden's *Eel* is a canoe-stern yawl that is exceedingly pretty with her graceful sheer, rounded topsides, and well-spooned, nicely matched ends. Her shoal draft results from the absence of keel, low deadrise bottom

fitted with a centerboard, and an unusual spade rudder that can be withdrawn into a trunk abaft a shallow skeg. Her sliding-gunter yawl rig looks appropriate and allows short spars. She should be stiff, with her generous waterline beam and full stern. Auxiliary propulsion is a pair of oars used while standing up and facing forward. For short distances, one oar would probably suffice if you held the tiller to one side. Construction is carvel planking, but she could be strip planked or cold molded.

The designer suggests a canvas hood and battens to shelter sleeping bags when overnighting, but I'd be tempted to add a small cuddy trunk with a round end forward and a single oval port on each side. With or without the cuddy, though, *Eel* is the kind of small boat that any sailor with even a modicum of taste would be mighty proud to own.

Plans from Yacht Designs *by William Garden, International Marine, 1977*

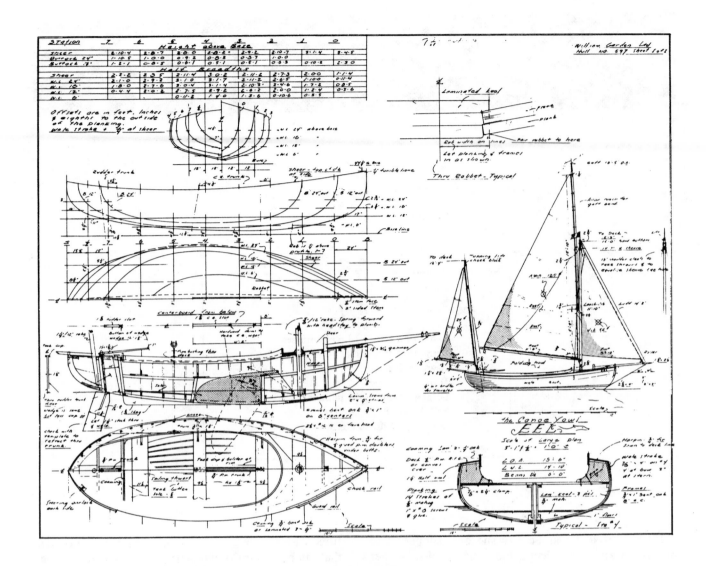

· 36 ·

Itatae

Length on Deck: 27 feet
Length on Waterline: 25 feet 4 inches
Beam: 9 feet 8 inches
Draft: 4 feet
Ballast: 2,500 pounds
Sail Area: 421 square feet
Designer: William Garden

In recent years, there has been a great revival of interest in cat-ketches and cat-schooners. Here is one with traditional lines that is much more handsome than some of the current crop. William Garden designed this double-ender, named *Itatae,* after what seems to have been a long, hard look at the Block Island boat.

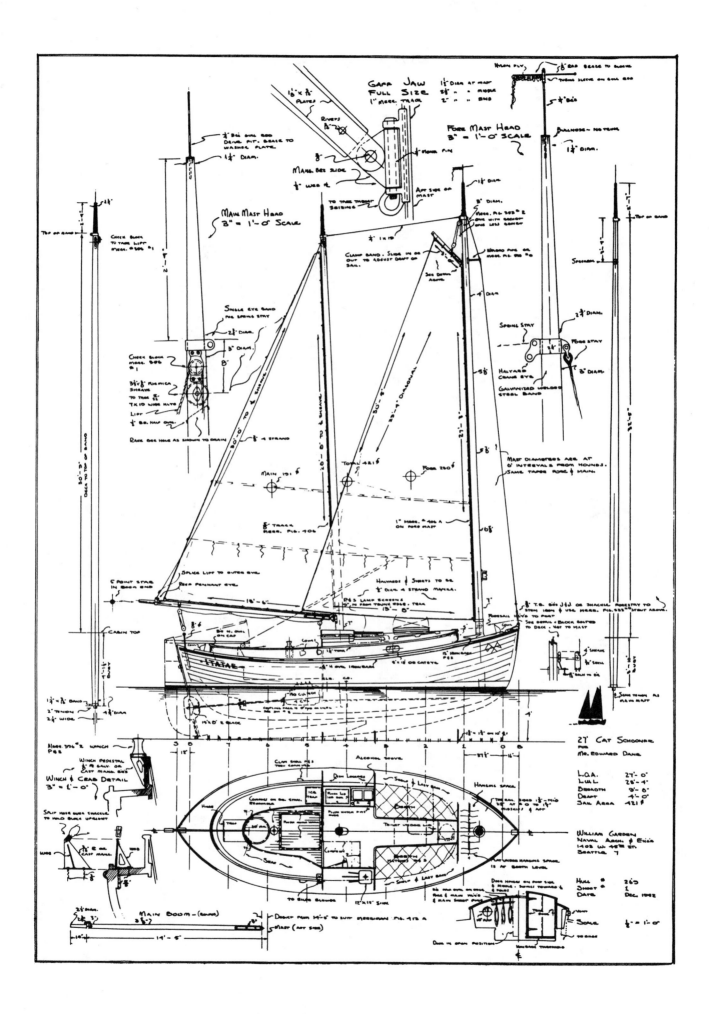

27' CAT SCHOONER
for
Mr. Edward Dane

L.O.A. .... 27'-0"
L.W.L. .... 25'-4"
BREADTH ...... 9'-0"
DRAFT .... 4'-0"
SAIL AREA .... 421☐

WILLIAM GARDEN
NAVAL ARCH. & ENGR.
1403 W. 46TH ST.
SEATTLE 7

HULL # 265
SHEET 1
DATE .... DEC. 1952

SCALE .... ½" = 1'-0"

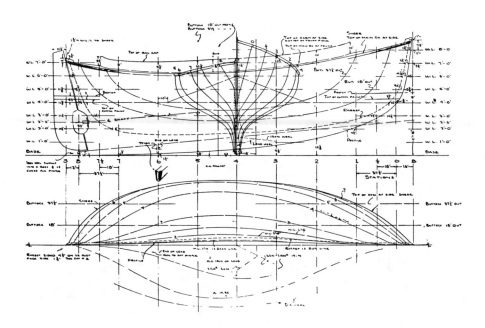

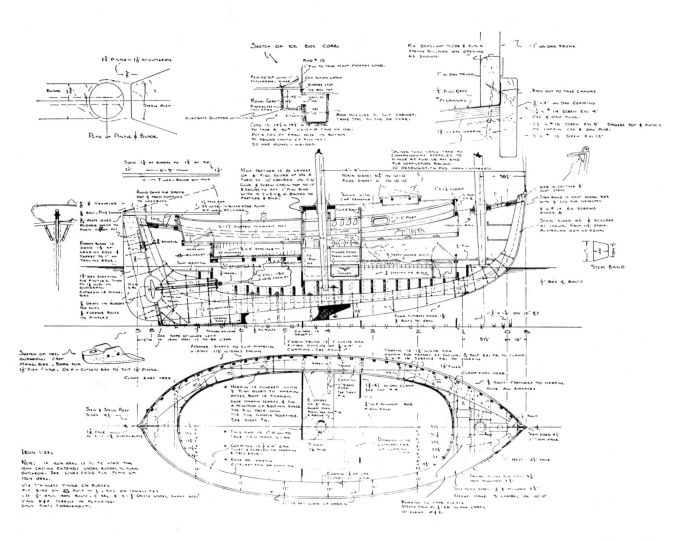

The advantages of *Itatae* are ease of handling, seakindliness, daysailing and short-range-cruising comfort, and, of course, eye-catching character. The long keel with some drag affords good lateral resistance with modest draft and good directional stability, while the broad champagne-glass sections offer a combination of stability with ease of motion and a reduction of wetted surface. Accommodations are limited, since a lot of space is allotted to the cockpit. Still there is room for a good-sized galley, two berths, and a concealed head.

The rig is well matched to the long keel, since the boat can sail under one sail with a tolerable helm. If the foresail were boomed, it could be self-tending and more easily reefed, but the overlap provides more power. Since there are no shrouds, the mast sections are fairly large, but they could be reduced with modern carbon-fiber spars now readily available. Although the sail area is not large, *Itatae* is capable of good speed in a breeze. This is verified by a run she once made of over 100 miles, averaging slightly better than 6½ knots.

Plans from Good Boats *by Roger C. Taylor, International Marine, 1977*

37

Porpoise

Length on Deck: 42 feet 4 inches
Length on Waterline: 33 feet 4 inches
Beam: 13 feet 4 inches
Draft: 5 feet 8 inches
Displacement: 34,000 pounds
Sail Area: 950 square feet
Designer: William Garden

The ketch *Porpoise,* designed by William Garden, is a rugged cruiser suitable for living aboard and long voyages, preferably in the trade-wind belts. In a very general way, she reminds me of Joshua Slocum's *Spray,* but *Porpoise* is fancier, a lot more comfortable, and safer with her deeper, heavily ballasted keel to extend her stability range. She's a distinguished-looking vessel with a bow that seems to challenge any head sea, although the sweeping sheer and high freeboard forward restrict visibility from the helm somewhat.

There are a variety of rigs and accommodations arrangements for the *Porpoise* hull. My own preference for long passages with a family or two couples would be the ketch rig with the below-decks arrangement that trades off the lazarette for a stateroom and private head aft. A nice feature in several arrangements is the sitting/dining area directly opposite the galley. The ketch rig is a good compromise between ease of handling, balance, and power. The foretriangle is not huge, but it is large enough for a good-sized jib and twins that will work well in the trades.

The designer says that his *Porpoise* designs have proven popular, and well over a hundred versions are sailing the seas. Construction is conventional carvel planking on bent oak frames. Despite the work of building such a large, heavy vessel, it is not surprising that some of these boats were home built. Boats like *Porpoise* are what dreams are made of.

Plans from Yacht Designs *by William Garden, International Marine, 1977*

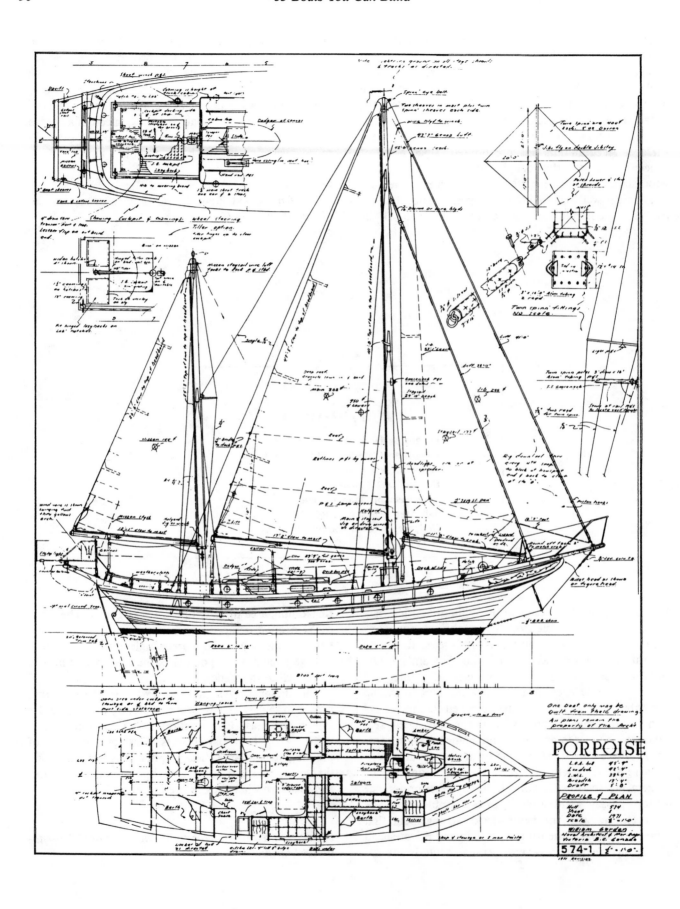

PORPOISE

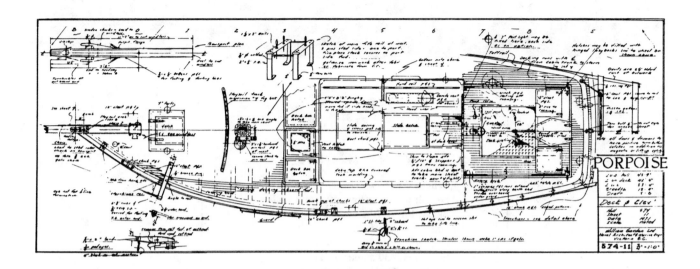

PORPOISE

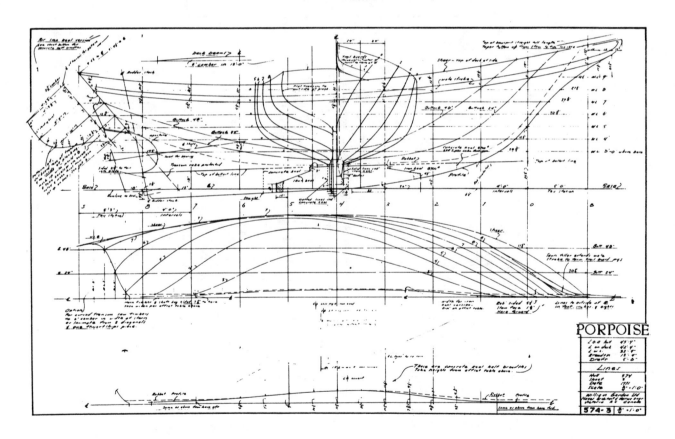

PORPOISE

THOMAS C. GILLMER

38

Blue Moon

Length on Deck: 22 feet 10 inches
Length on Waterline: 19 feet 8 inches
Beam: 8 feet 7 inches
Draft: 4 feet 1 inch
Displacement: 8,000 pounds
Sail Area: 430 square feet
Designer: Thomas C. Gillmer

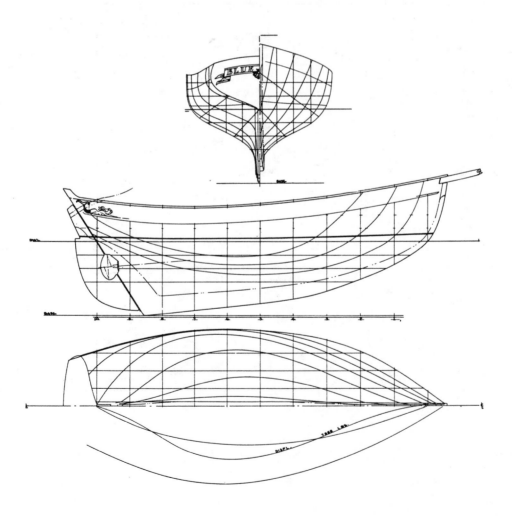

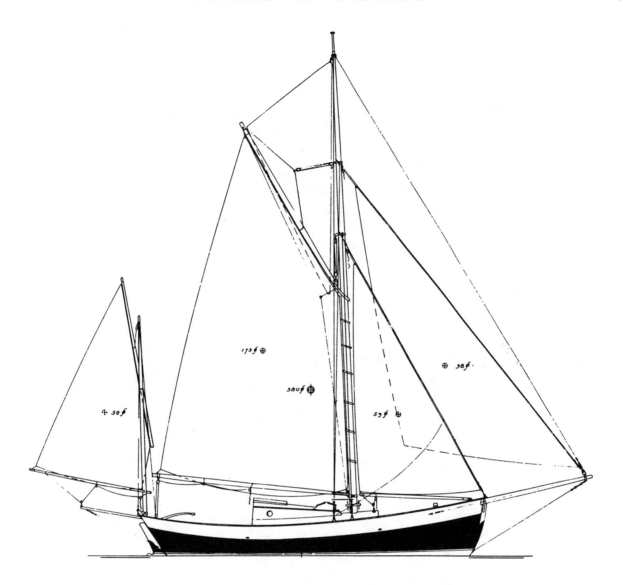

Thomas C. Gillmer of Annapolis, Maryland, is not only a gifted yacht architect, but also a ship designer, former professor at the U.S. Naval Academy, director of a model testing tank, workboat historian, and author of several technical books on naval architecture. Perhaps he is best known by the yachting public as designer of the Seawind ketch, the first fiberglass boat to make a circumnavigation.

The 23-foot *Blue Moon* is a yacht Professor Gillmer designed based on a notable workboat known as the Falmouth quay punt, a seaworthy ferry and cargo carrier that was used to serve vessels anchored in the roadstead at Falmouth, England. Despite her rather heavy wood construction, which gives her additional seakindliness and power, she is a lively sailer. Said to be a good ghoster in light airs, *Blue Moon* is also no slouch in a breeze, and, according to Tom Gillmer, she sails well to windward. Her beam and full lines aft make her quite stiff.

Her cabin is the raised-deck type, which provides extra space below. To keep water from slopping into the cockpit, I'd want to install a bit of coaming at the aft end of the raised deck and to pipe the scupper at that location into the cockpit rather than lead it through the rail. (The cockpit would be self-bailing.) The layout below is cleverly arranged to provide a full galley, a semiprivate head, and two good berths.

Plans from More Good Boats *by Roger C. Taylor, International Marine, 1979*

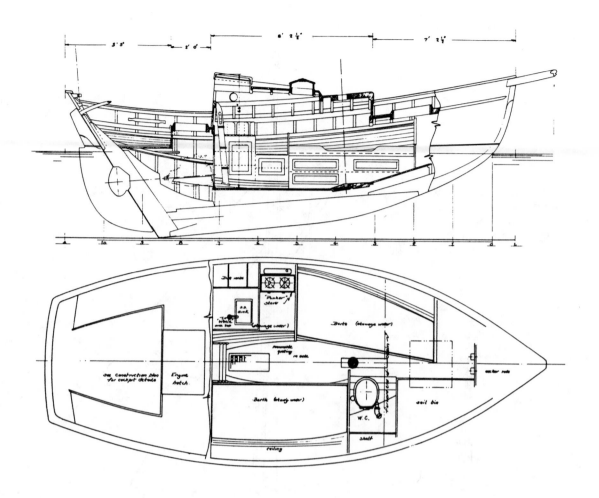

39

Calypso

Length on Deck: 35 feet 9 inches
Length on Waterline: 31 feet 3 inches
Beam: 11 feet
Draft: 5 feet 1 inch
Displacement: 20,000 pounds
Sail Area: 827 square feet
Designer: Thomas C. Gillmer

The 36-foot ketch *Calypso,* another Gillmer design, is somewhat similar to *Blue Moon* (design No. 38), but larger and differently rigged. In some respects, I prefer *Calypso* for her greater room below, higher freeboard amidships, and slightly flatter sheer with less-prominent bowsprit steeve. *Calypso* too behaves well under sail, and her long keel and symmetrical lines give her a steady helm. The sharp entrance with generous flare forward

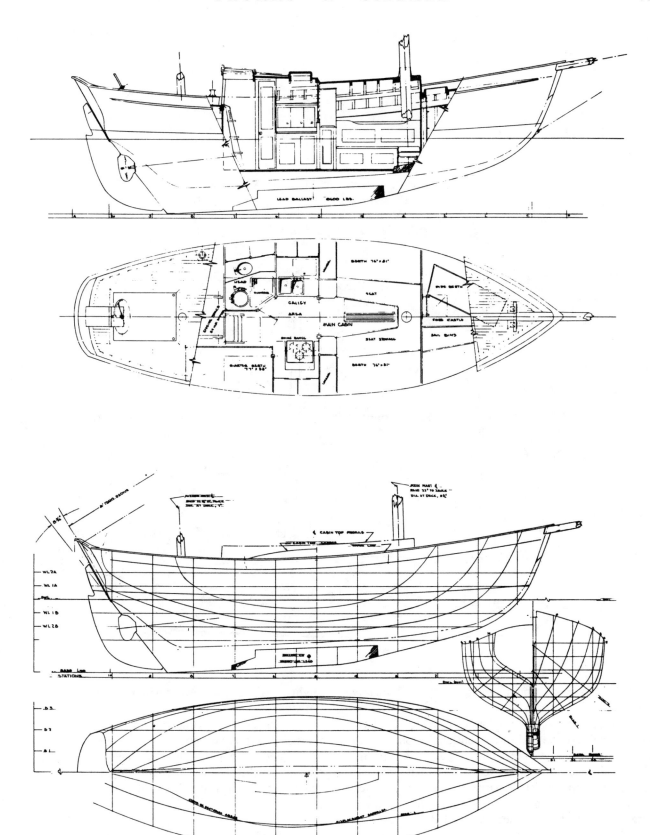

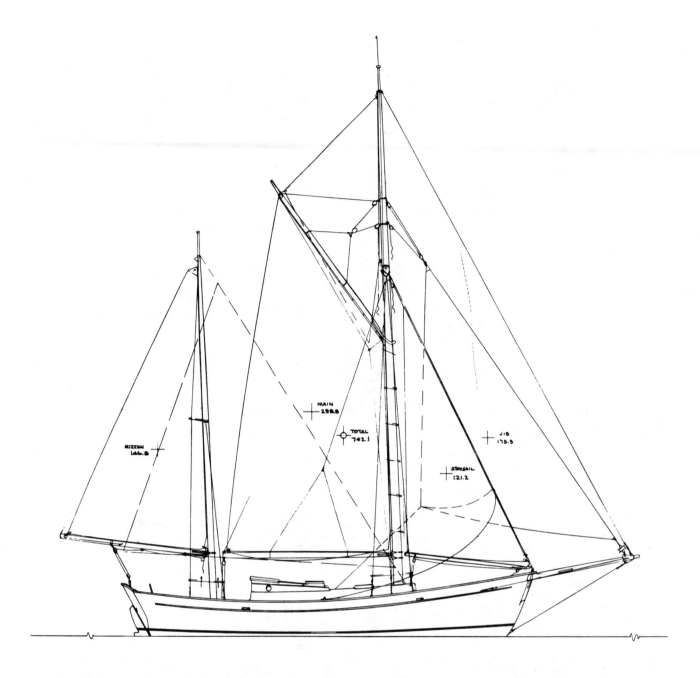

allows her to power through head seas with a reasonably dry foredeck.

Actually, there are two versions of *Calypso*. The later one, shown here, has a less-conventional cabin and an improved rig. I might prefer the original cabin trunk, which had several portholes, to the new high-crowned, flush-deck cabin, which is darker below and less well ventilated, but the new plan is suited for northern waters. The new layout places the head aft and provides a fixed saloon table and a separate forepeak for either a boatswain's locker or quarters for a youthful hand. I

might want a larger forward hatch for easier access and sail stowage.

The new rig with its double headsails and large mizzen staysail offers good versatility for a variety of conditions. The main gaff could be nicely vanged to the mizzen masthead. Consideration might be given to a grooved foil-type roller jib, which would reduce luff sag.

Plans from More Good Boats *by Roger C. Taylor, International Marine, 1979*

JAY HANNA ET AL.

• 40 •

Pemaquid

Length on Deck: 25 feet
Length on Waterline: 21 feet 4 inches
Beam: 8 feet 8 inches
Draft: 4 feet 5 inches
Sail Area: 432 square feet
Designer: Abdon K. Carter

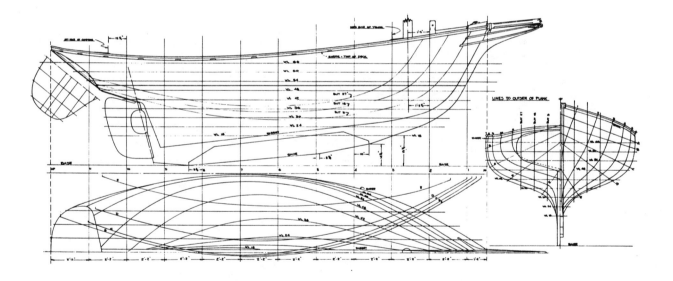

No book that features traditional designs would be complete without the plans of a Friendship sloop, the classic deep-keel fishing sloop originating in the late 1800s and identified with the town of Friendship, Maine. Primarily because of its appealing looks and character, it has a small cult of worshippers, and there is a Friendship Sloop Society that sponsors an annual regatta.

Although not intended for deep-sea voyaging, the small vessel worked offshore as well as inshore in all kinds of weather. Howard Blackburn, a fisherman who had lost all his fingers, crossed the Atlantic singlehanded in a type closely related to the Friendship.

The sloop *Pemaquid,* featured here, is based on a Friendship sloop built by Abdon Carter in 1914, as

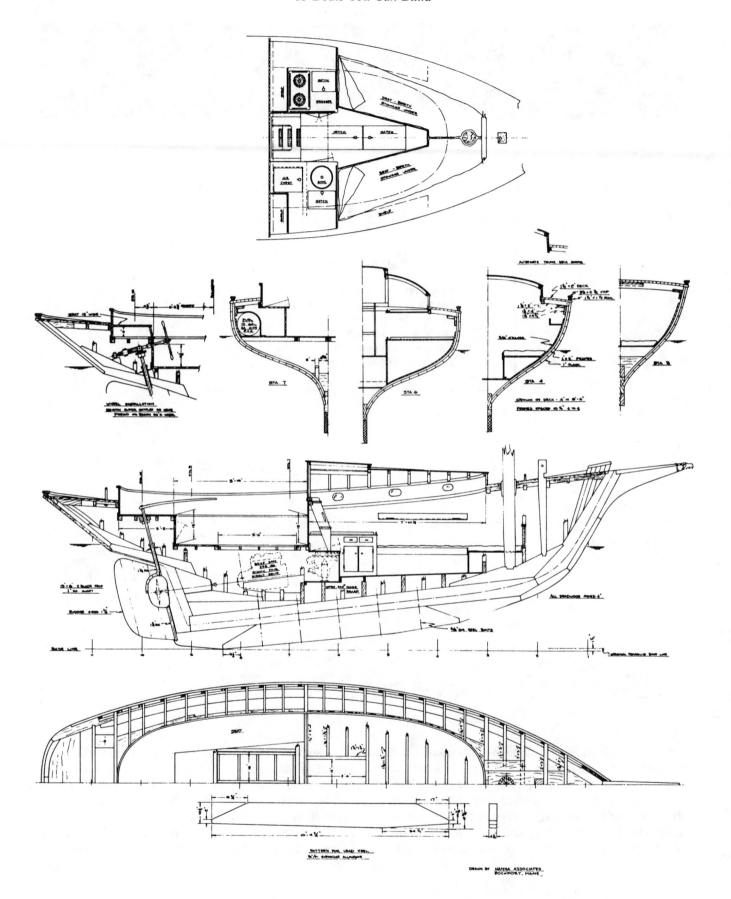

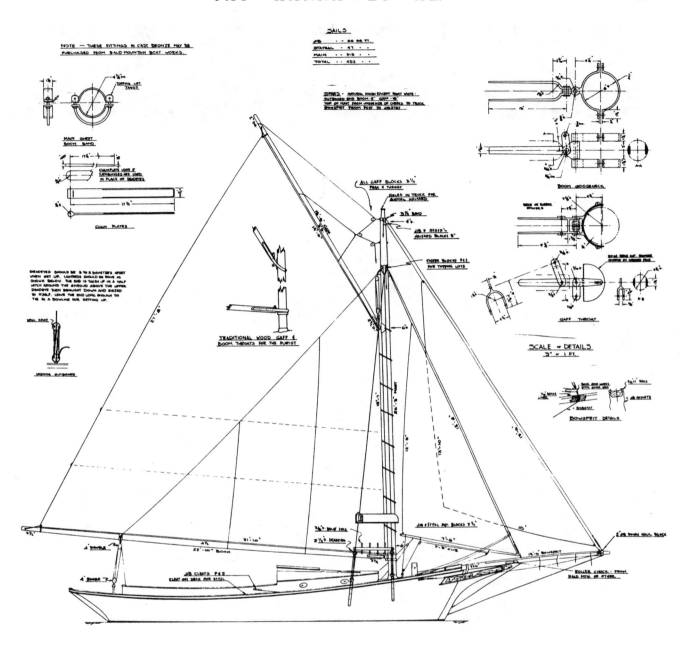

recorded by Howard I. Chapelle and Charles G. MacGregor. Her plans were drawn by Jay Hanna of Rockport, Maine. She has the typical clipper bow with hollow entrance for easing her generous beam through head seas, sweeping sheer with high freeboard forward for dryness, and the raked oval transom, which prevents sheet fouling and affords some reserve buoyancy aft. *Pemaquid* has the hollow garboards typical of the type, but whereas the original boat carried inside ballast, she has been given outside ballast for superior stability and greater safety. A desirable feature is the upward slope of the keel end so that the boat will ground on her ballast.

Her cabin is small, but cozy and adequate for two, and it leaves space for a sizable cockpit. Certain details such as the trail boards and billet head, make this boat unusually attractive.

Under sail, the Friendship sloop excels on a reach, provided it is not allowed to heel too much. It is not close-winded, but Chapelle argued that some, by virtue of their power, could beat a heavily ballasted narrow boat to windward in a real gale of wind.

Plans from Enduring Friendships, *edited by Al Roberts, International Marine, 1970*

L. FRANCIS HERRESHOFF

41

H-14

Length: 14 feet
Beam: 4 feet 6 inches
Weight: 300 pounds
Sail Area: 75 square feet
Designer: L. Francis Herreshoff

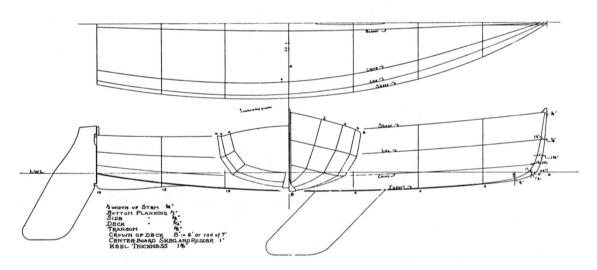

½ WIDTH OF STEM ¾"
BOTTOM PLANKING ½"
SIDE   ⅜"
DECK   ⁵⁄₁₆"
TRANSOM   ⅝"
CROWN OF DECK 8" in 6' or rad of 7'
CENTER-BOARD SKEG AND RUDDER 1"
KEEL THICKNESS 1⅛"

L. Francis Herreshoff built up a following that almost could be called reverential. This devotion continues not only because of his sensible and very artistic designs, an outstanding example being the famous ketch *Ticonderoga,* but also because of his skillful, perceptive writing.

The H-14 is L. Francis's concept of a smart sailing dinghy that can be used as a junior trainer, yet is roomy enough for two adults. Another objective was that the boat be inexpensive and easy to build. To this end, he adopted a two-chine hull form and dory-type construction, which he described in his book *Sensible Cruising Designs*. The boat is intended for dry storage, and although she weighs 300 pounds, Herreshoff claimed she could easily be hauled out on a ramp or trailer.

The rig is the designer's idea of an improved sliding gunter. The sail can be lowered rapidly, and when it is reefed, there is no bare spar sticking up above the headboard. The boat can be quickly rigged or unrigged, and no spar is extremely long.

Some nice features are the roomy cockpit, the decking and washboard, the rowing thwart, and the raked daggerboard, which can absorb some shock when the boat runs aground. I would want some flotation, enough to keep the top of the daggerboard trunk above the water when the boat is swamped.

Plans from Sensible Cruising Designs *by L. Francis Herreshoff, International Marine, 1973*

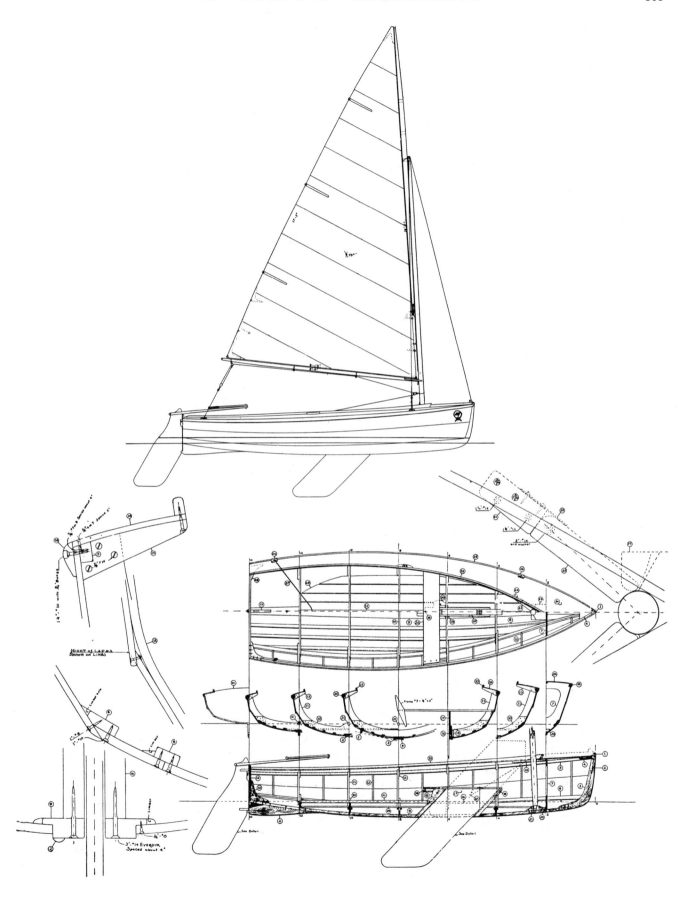

· 42 ·

Centerboard Knockabout

Length on Deck: 17 feet
Length on Waterline: 14 feet 4 inches
Beam: 5 feet
Draft: 4 inches
Sail Area: 124 square feet
Designer: L. Francis Herreshoff

There's nothing much under the water to slow down this 17-foot knockabout designed by L. Francis Herreshoff. She could all but sail on a dewdrop if a kick-up rudder could be fitted. She should also be quick to plane and extremely fast in most conditions, provided you could hold her flat. To this end, I'd want some hiking straps and a long tiller extension.

You might want to modernize the sloop rig, at least

raise the gooseneck a bit. Although the club-footed jib is handy because it is self-tending, most owners would want to show off the boat's speed, and she'd probably be faster with a slightly larger loose-footed jib. If you wanted even more speed, you could install a bendy mast and running backstays, but, of course, "souping up" the rig trades off some handiness.

The hull is fairly symmetrical for a planing boat, but

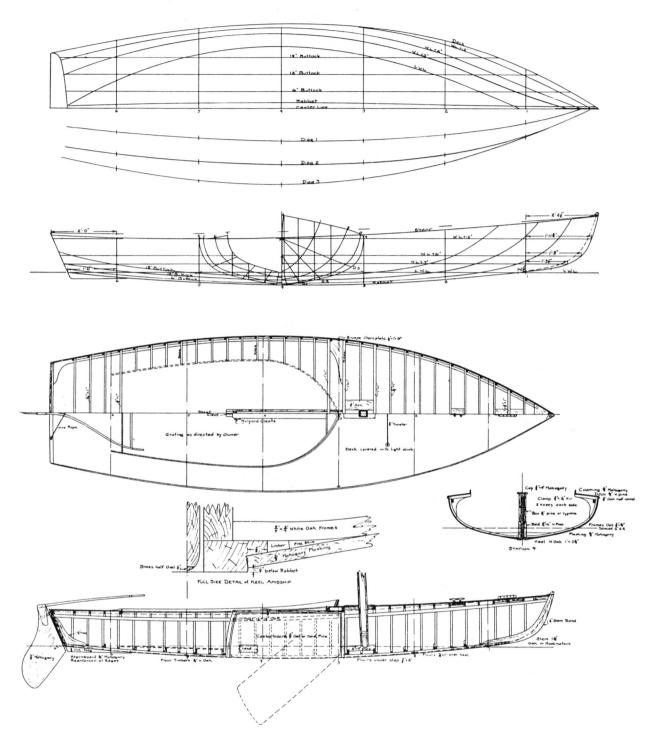

there is enough fullness aft for reasonable bearing and crew support. The bow is a marvel, balancing the requirements of good looks, long sailing length, and the ability to cut through a chop without unnecessary wetness.

This boat can afford plenty of fun, not only because of her smart sailing ability and speed, but also because of her 4-inch draft, which allows easy beaching and marsh crawling. But don't forget to ship your rudder.

Plans from Sensible Cruising Designs *by L. Francis Herreshoff, International Marine, 1973*

43

Prudence

Length on Deck: 22 feet 9 inches
Length on Waterline: 19 feet 9 inches
Beam: 8 feet
Draft: 3 feet
Sail Area: 292 square feet
Designer: L. Francis Herreshoff

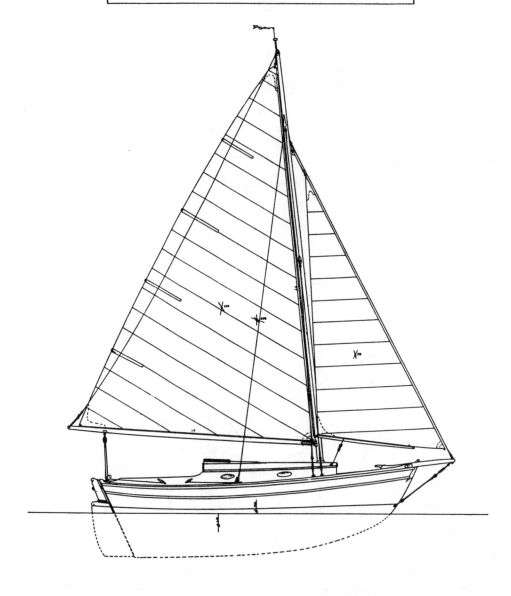

Prudence, designed by L. Francis Herreshoff, is a handsome tabloid cruiser. Her moderate draft makes her suitable for gunkhole cruising.

The foredeck should keep reasonably dry because of the freeboard forward and flare just under the rail. Wineglass transoms do not always afford great bearing at low angles of heel, but they keep large transoms from dragging, and they are certainly easy on the eye.

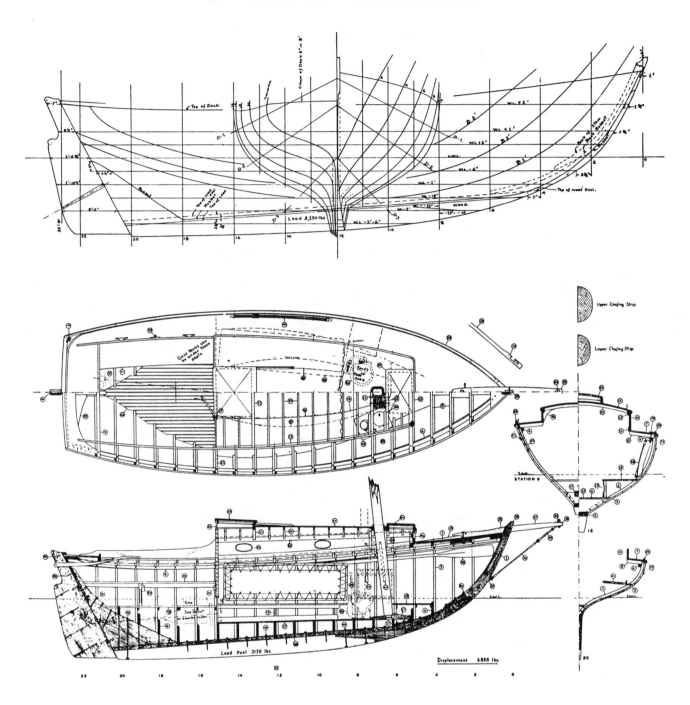

A snug cabin provides reasonable comfort for two, and the head up forward is in the most private location. The engine specified is a Gray Sea Scout, though the designer said that he preferred no engine at all. The rig appears to be a handy one, though running backstays are necessary for forestay tension.

Prudence appears to be a smart sailing, versatile boat,

suitable for just about any service except long offshore passages. A lovely painting of her appears on the dust jacket of Herreshoff's book *Sensible Cruising Designs*.

Plans from Sensible Cruising Designs *by L. Francis Herreshoff, International Marine, 1973*

· **44** ·

Rozinante

Length on Deck: 28 feet
Length on Waterline: 24 feet
Beam: 6 feet 4 inches
Draft: 3 feet 9 inches
Displacement: 6,600 pounds
Sail Area: 348 square feet
Designer: L. Francis Herreshoff

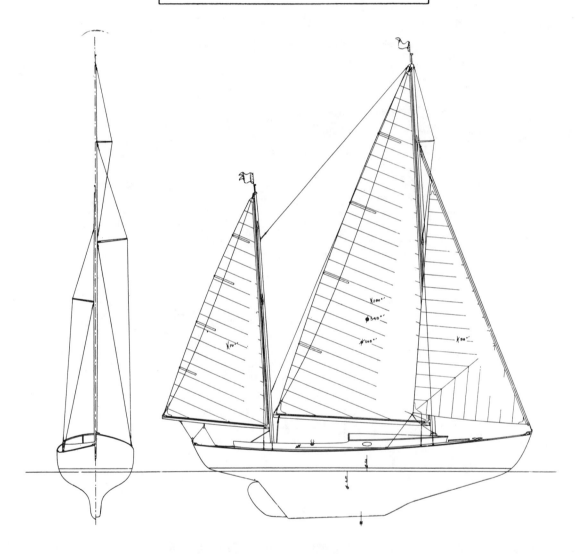

Like the *Eel* (design No. 35), *Rozinante,* designed by L. Francis Herreshoff, is a canoe yawl. Many years ago these boats generated a lot of interest, at first when Englishman John MacGregor popularized cruising in his so-called Rob Roy canoe yawls and then when Albert Strange introduced his larger and more sea-worthy canoe-stern yachts. Today there seems to be a revival of interest in such craft, perhaps partly as a re-action against the repetition and lack of beauty in many modern mass-produced stock designs.

Rozinante is one of America's best-known and pretti-est canoe yawls. She is not a true gunkholer like most,

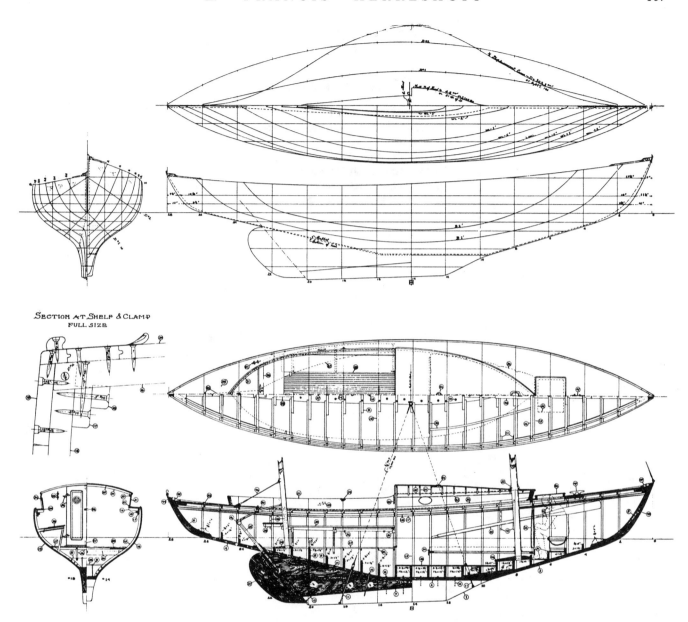

SECTION AT SHELF & CLAMP
FULL SIZE

but still she draws only 3 feet 9 inches, and the ballasted keel makes her a good sea boat. It also provides sufficient lateral plane for quite good windward ability. There is a *Rozinante* in my home waters, and I am always impressed with the way she sails. Her speed comes from a low-wetted-surface and a narrow, light, and easily moved hull form with ample waterline length. The symmetry of her lines, moderately long keel, and divided rig allow her to track and balance well. The rig, which might actually be called a ketch, has a low center of effort to counteract any lack of initial stability caused by the narrow beam. The hull can also be propelled by oars. Plank-on-frame construction is light but strong.

Although accommodations are meager, there are two adequate berths, and some privacy is provided by having the head up forward and a curtain that closes off the forepeak. As for adding a doghouse for a galley, L. Francis has written scornfully, "If you like eating better than sailing, you should stay home and have a barbecue in the backyard."

Plans from Sensible Cruising Designs *by L. Francis Herreshoff, International Marine, 1973*

· 45 ·

Meadow Lark

Length on Deck: 33 feet
Length on Waterline: 31 feet 10 inches
Beam: 8 feet 1½ inches
Draft: 1 foot 3 inches
Displacement: 8,000 pounds
Sail Area: 456 square feet
Designer: L. Francis Herreshoff

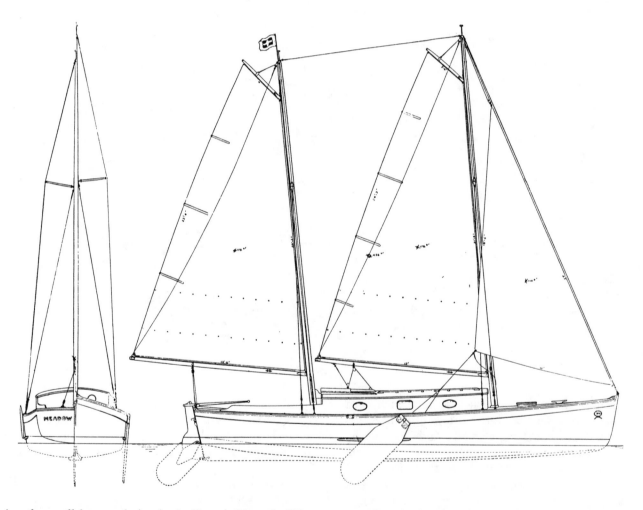

Another well-known design by L. Francis Herreshoff is his *Meadow Lark*. She is ideal for carefree cruising in thin-water areas such as those found along the Florida and Gulf coasts, Albemarle Sound, and Chesapeake Bay. Her modified sharpie hull draws a mere 15 inches, which is reason enough for her form, but L. Francis

wrote that she is shaped principally to make construction easy. Obviously, her conventional plank-on-frame construction is simplified by her hard chines and the absence of extreme curves. But notice how the sides and particularly the bottom are slightly rounded. This improves appearance, strengthens the hull, and inhibits

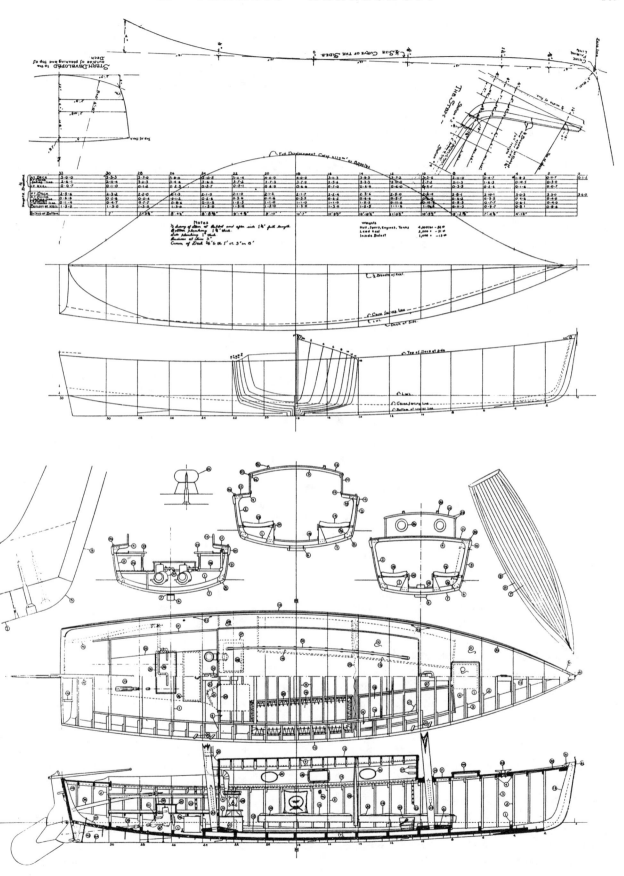

pounding. The chine is kept well below the waterline to prevent slapping when the boat is at anchor or sailing in a small chop.

Meadow Lark is a fairly fast boat despite her short rig. It is important to keep the sail area low because her stability range is limited. The short gaffs provide reasonable sail area, yet make handling easy with their light weight and single halyards. Leeboards have the advantage over a centerboard in greater room below, a stronger hull for beaching, and avoidance of jamming a centerboard slot with shells or gravel when grounding. A drawback is that you have to tend leeboards when coming about, and they often attract flotsam.

There is more room below than you might think. Two cabins, each with a pair of practical pipe berths, are divided by a curtain. The galley and a coal- or wood-burning Shipmate stove are aft, where, with the companionway hatch open, headroom is limited only by the stars.

The designer wrote, *"Meadow Lark* is a suitable name for this craft as she could venture inland and, you might say, skim over the marshes and meadows as the joyful bird of the same name does over many of our fields which border the Atlantic."

Plans from Sensible Cruising Designs *by L. Francis Herreshoff, International Marine, 1973*

· 46 ·

Nereia

Length on Deck: 36 feet
Length on Waterline: 31 feet 9 inches
Beam: 11 feet
Draft: 5 feet 3 inches
Displacement: 24,000 pounds
Sail Area: 673 square feet
Designer: L. Francis Herreshoff

A design that is typical of the work one associates with L. Francis Herreshoff is the beautiful ketch *Nereia*. With her sweeping sheerline, clipper bow, fine entrance, low freeboard, raised quarter rail, long cabin trunk, and boldly raked masts, she reminds me of Herreshoff's famous *Ticonderoga*. Of course, there are many differences between the two. The smaller *Nereia* has a different stern and underbody, but the relationship is there.

Nereia is very full at the garboards, a feature that can be detrimental to windward performance, but in this case upwind ability is retained by the ample draft and lateral plane. The fullness reduces wetted surface and allows a deeper cabin sole so that ample headroom can be had without raising the freeboard or the cabin trunk.

The rig is modest but sufficient for all conditions except beating in light airs. I would not like to have to thread a large masthead jib between the two forestays when tacking. The low, spread-out sail area together with ample ballast makes the boat stiff and easy to handle in a blow. Notice that the plans do not even show a means of reefing.

Her wood construction is conventional plank on frame, but a somewhat unusual detail is that the garboards are rabbeted into the lead keel. The designer feels that this is a way to prevent leaking at the garboards, since the lead won't swell like wood.

About the only thing *Nereia* lacks below is a chart table, but the navigator could use the cabin table. The lift-up berths in the saloon are most practical, but if I had L. Francis Herreshoff's art on the underside of the berth (as shown on the cabin plan), I'd cut it out, frame it, and hang it in my living room.

Plans from Sensible Cruising Designs *by L. Francis Herreshoff, International Marine, 1973*

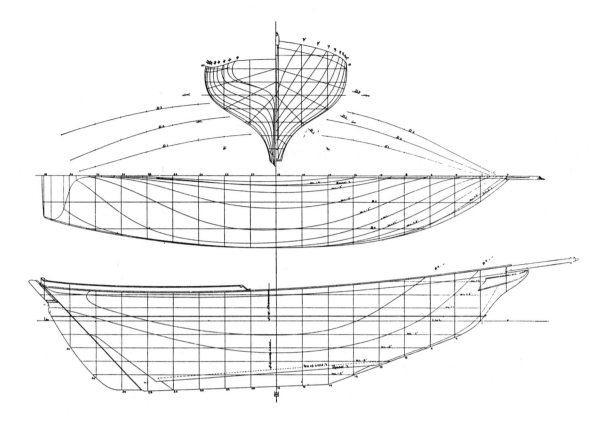

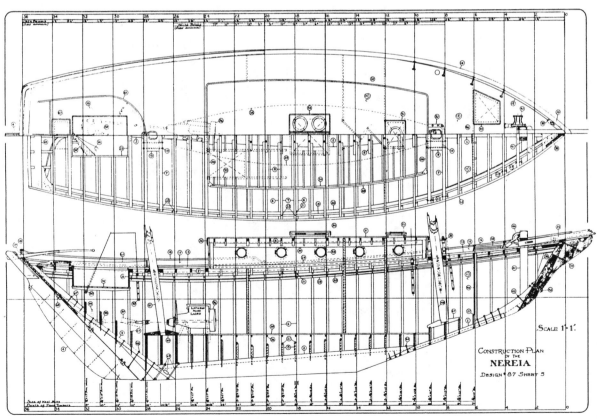

CONSTRUCTION PLAN
OF THE
NEREIA
DESIGN *87 SHEET 5

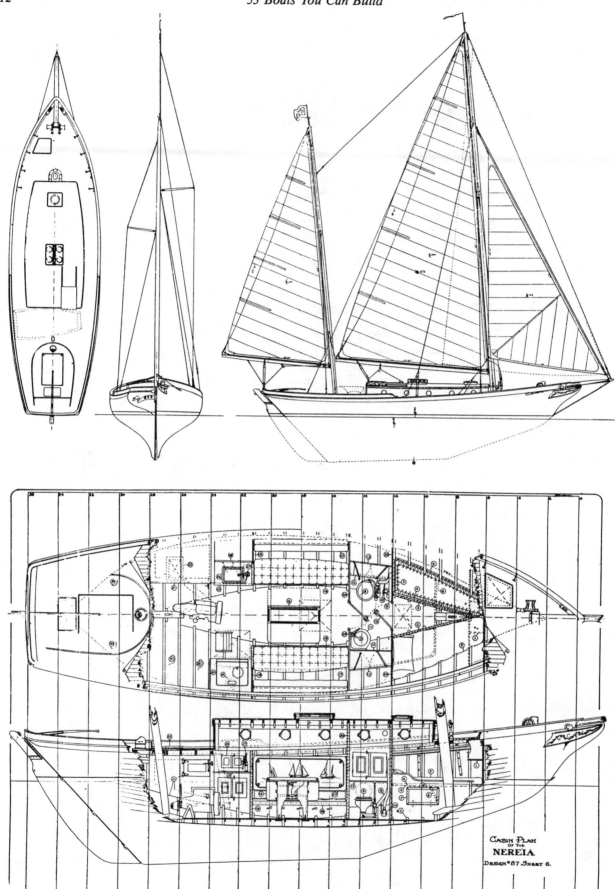

CABIN PLAN
OF THE
NEREIA
DESIGN #87 SHEET 6.

AL MASON

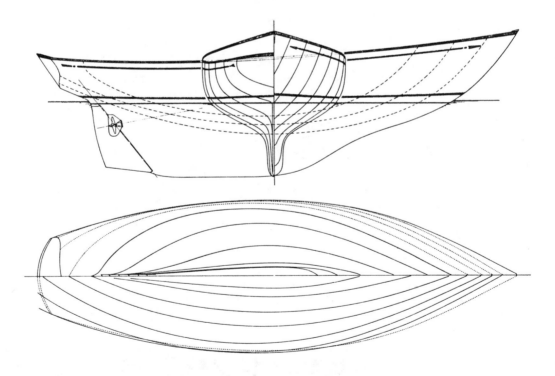

· 47 ·

Mason 31

Length on Deck: 31 feet
Length on Waterline: 22 feet 11 inches
Beam: 9 feet 4 inches
Draft: 4 feet 8 inches
Displacement: 10,400 pounds
Sail Area: 426 square feet
Designer: Alvin Mason

Al Mason is a seasoned naval architect who has practiced his profession with the leading yacht design firms of John G. Alden, Philip L. Rhodes, and Sparkman and Stephens. For many years, he has been practicing on his own in California. He is noted for his conservative, handsome yachts, which are always beautifully drawn.

The Mason 31 is a fine example of this talented designer's work. She is a handsome boat with nicely

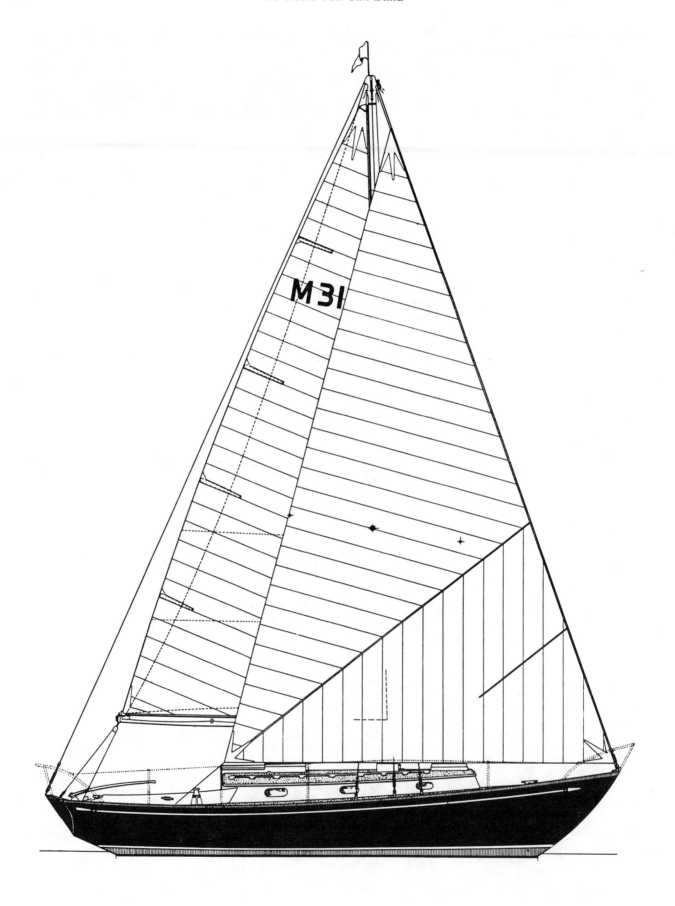

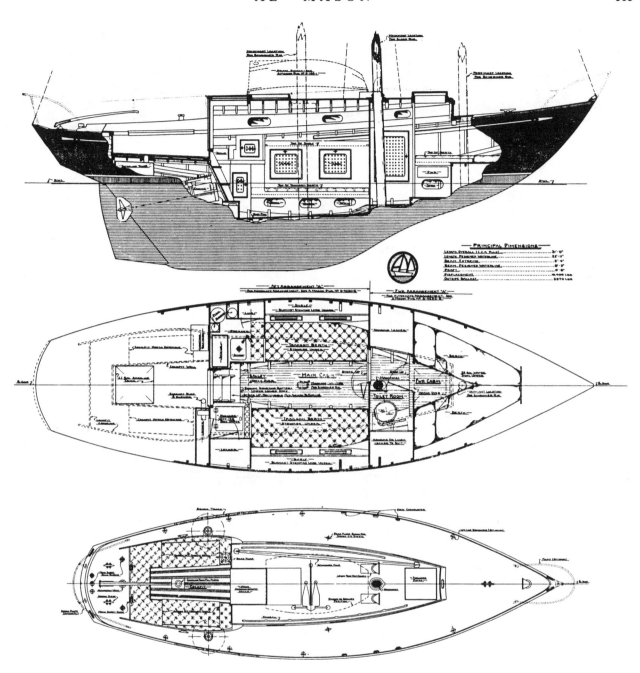

balanced ends, a pronounced sheer, a high bow with moderate freeboard aft, and a low cabin trunk. Her conservative design, with no element in any way extreme, assures seakindliness, steadiness, dryness, and forgiveness.

Although not as fast as a modern, relatively light displacement racing cruiser, the Mason 31 is no slouch as a sailer. She is smart, directionally stable, and quite stiff. The outboard shrouds prevent pointing high, but she goes to windward with enthusiasm. The designer offers a choice of two rigs: a functional, easy-to-handle sloop or a schooner rig. The second is less practical, but it is very appealing aesthetically and can provide a lot of reaching power in light airs.

The layout below is standard and eminently sensible, with a number of features not seen everyday, such as the double-hinged door, berth foot well, dustpan, and well-ventilated lockers. The designer is noted for his meticulous attention to details.

Plans from Choice Yacht Designs *by Richard Henderson, International Marine, 1979*

C.W. PAINE

48

Frances

Length on Deck: 25 feet 9½ inches
Length on Waterline: 21 feet 3 inches
Beam: 8 feet
Draft: 3 feet 10 inches
Displacement: 6,800 pounds
Sail Area: 337 square feet
Designer: C.W. Paine

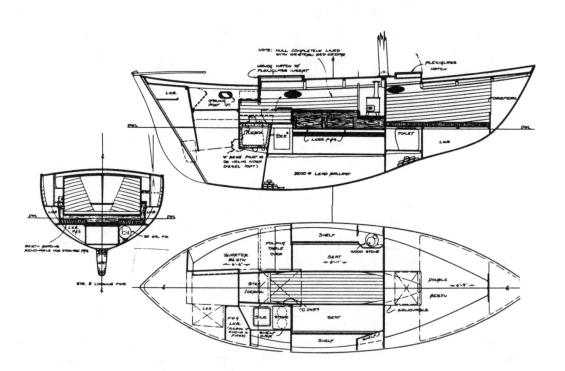

Compared with many of the veteran designers in this book, C.W. "Chuck" Paine, the designer of *Frances,* is a youngster; yet he is highly experienced, and his work has a proclivity toward the traditional. Even though he is most often associated with full-keel and double-ended designs, this designer is a racing skipper and has turned out some fast boats for the Richard Carter design firm. Paine designs, whether racers or cruisers, have a reputa-

tion for being smart sailers, and *Frances* is no exception.

Designed for Paine's own use in 1975, *Frances* has been a great success and has proven particularly popular in Europe. She is built of fiberglass by Thomas D.C. Morris at Southwest Harbor, Maine, and the boat can be had at various stages of construction.

With her shapely ends, attractive sheer, and low cabin, *Frances* presents an exceedingly handsome pro-

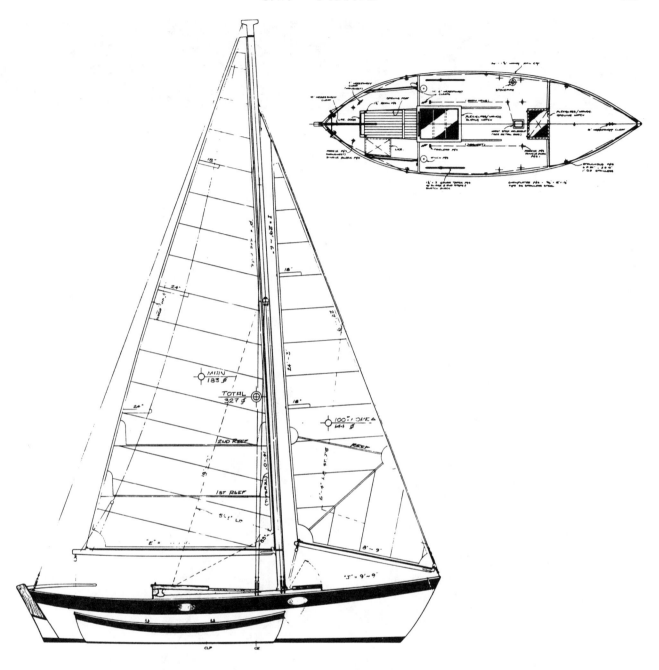

file. She has fairly slack bilges for easy motion and low wetted surface, a fairly fine entrance for good progress in head seas, and tightly radiused garboards for windward ability. Her tall, efficient sloop rig also helps give her good performance to windward. The seven-eighths foretriangle makes her an easy boat to handle in a fresh breeze.

The designer wisely resisted any temptation to give her a high cabin trunk that might detract from her looks. All that is needed on a boat this size is comfortable sitting headroom, and this is achieved very well with the raised deck. A large sliding hatch allows standing when you feel the urge. There are some clever details below, and the plans deserve careful study.

For a small boat, *Frances* is quite seaworthy and could go almost anywhere. If you haven't time to sail her there, however, she could te taken over land, as her 8-foot beam allows trailering.

Plans from 60 Boat Designs for Power and Sail from National Fisherman, *International Marine, 1981*

49

Wild Duck

Length on Deck: 26 feet
Length on Waterline: 23 feet 2 inches
Beam: 9 feet 2 inches
Draft: 4 feet
Sail Area: 350 square feet
Designer: Murray G. Peterson

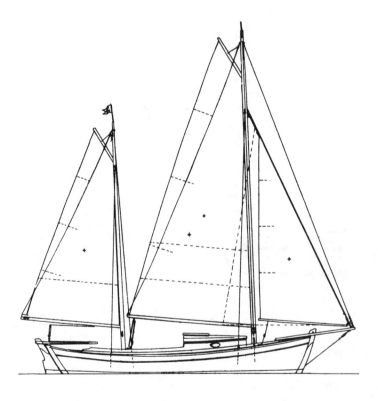

Another 26-foot double-ender is *Wild Duck,* but she is quite different from *Frances* (design No. 48). The *Wild Duck* design has been strongly influenced by the beamy Block Island cowhorn, and she might be considered a workboat modified for yachting. Her designer is the late Murray J. Peterson, who was an alumnus of the famous John Alden firm, and who is noted for his beautiful coaster-type yachts, especially his sturdy schooners.

Wild Duck has an exceptionally seakindly hull. The

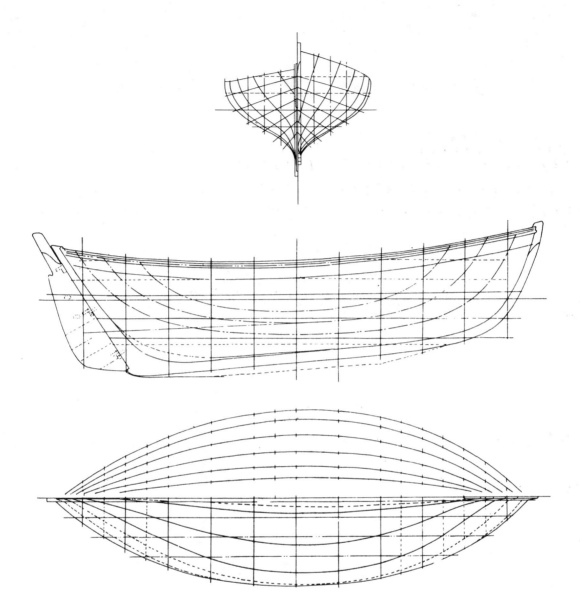

slack bilges inhibit pounding and assure an easy rolling motion. She has some initial tenderness but stiffens on heeling, for the beam increases rapidly as she knocks down. Her flaring topsides also provide dryness and good deck space. The lines are amazingly symmetrical, and this indicates some lack of power aft but good directional stability.

The ketch rig with short gaffs affords easy handling, keeps the masts low, and nicely matches the long keel. In a strong breeze, she should balance well under jib and mizzen or mainsail alone. She should be a very satisfactory sailer if you don't expect her to beat to windward like a modern racing-cruiser.

Of the boat's accommodations, a recent owner has written: "The cabin is that rare design which has comfortable space for two." The cockpit is divided to keep the crew out of the helmsman's way and to put their weight amidships.

Despite her workboat heritage, *Wild Duck* is finely finished; she was beautifully built of high-quality woods by the late Malcolm Brewer of Camden, Maine. She's a real little gem.

Plans from Good Boats *by Roger C. Taylor, International Marine, 1977*

FENWICK C. WILLIAMS

• 50 •

21-foot Catboat

Length on Deck: 20 feet 7 inches
Length on Waterline: 20 feet
Beam: 9 feet 6 inches
Draft: 2 feet
Sail Area: 324 square feet
Designer: Fenwick C. Williams

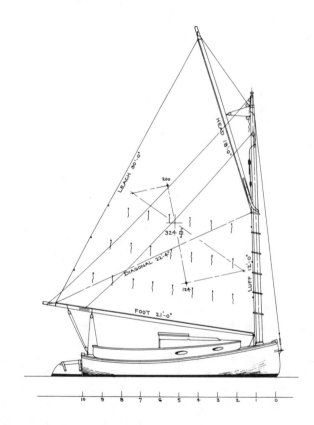

Fenwick C. Williams is another naval architect who worked for John Alden beginning in the 1920s, and later he did outstanding work for C. Raymond Hunt. Williams has designed a great number of catboats in his day, and this 21-footer is a fine example of his work.

She is quite similar to a Cape Cod cat of the late 1800s, but fuller in the bow. Not long ago, the designer wrote me, "How I detested the fine forward, fat aft hull form." Of course, any catboat must be fairly fine forward to move her enormous beam through steep seas,

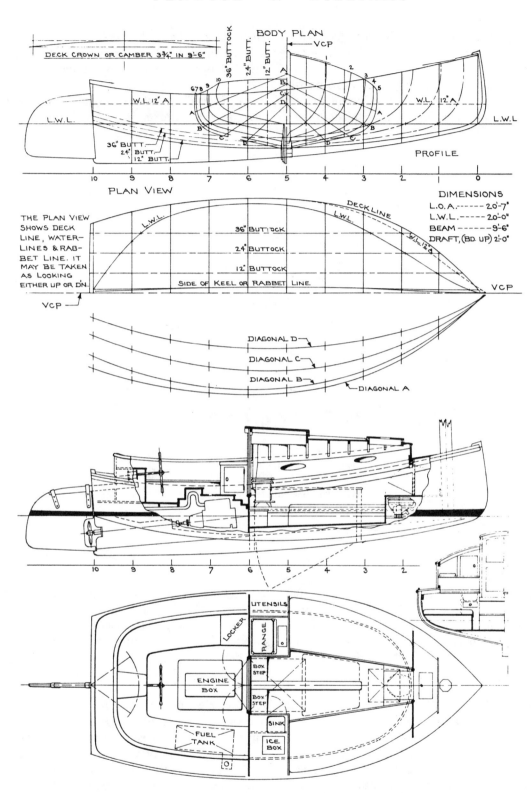

and this Williams boat has a hollow entrance; but the load waterline has a shoulder forward, and the hull is more balanced than most.

The boat's sheer is what the designer calls "lively,"

and this feature, together with her low freeboard aft, high coaming, and retroussé stem, gives her a most appealing, nostalgic look. The cabin is most satisfactory for two. About the only objection might be some lack of privacy with respect to the head, but the designer says there seems to be one obvious place for it, and he suggests a curtain.

The gaff sail is peaked up fairly high. This gaff position seems to control sail twist, allow sufficient space between head of sail and mast for fine adjustment of the halyards, and keep the center of effort forward to alleviate weather helm. A wheel eases steering and permits full use of the cockpit when under sail.

Plans from The Catboat Book, *edited by John M. Leavens, International Marine, 1973*

· 51 ·

28-foot Catboat

Length on Deck: 28 feet
Beam: 12 feet 6 inches
Draft: 3 feet 2 inches
Sail Area: 656 square feet
Designer: Fenwick C. Williams

One prominent aficionado of catboats claims that Fenwick Williams designed more cats than any living person. Well, here is another example of Williams's work, a 28-footer designed in 1931, when he was with John Alden. The original boat built to this design, named *Molly II,* was lost in a storm according to Alden records.

Compared with Williams's 21-footer (design No. 50), this boat is a lot more roomy both in the cockpit and down below. This size boat allows an enclosed head. There are also two more bunks, since the after berth has a back that swings up to form an upper berth. The seat opposite the after berths, next to the coal stove, would be a snug place to sit on a cold evening early or late in the boating season. The engine box in the cockpit makes a nice table in fair weather.

No lines are included with these plans, but a section drawing shows a fairly hard bilge for good initial stability, but without a sharp turn that would make frame bending difficult, give the boat a wall-sided appearance, and cause a more jerky roll in beam seas. She has about a 12-degree angle of deadrise, which the designer feels balances seaworthiness, performance, and initial stability for this type of boat. Aesthetically, this cat is not quite as pleasing, in my opinion, as the 21-footer, because of her slightly straighter sheer and stem line, but she is still a handsome boat and eminently functional. She can comfortably carry a large daysailing party or four for cruising and can be gotten underway, sailed, and secured with a minimum of effort.

Plans from The Catboat Book, *edited by John M. Leavens, International Marine, 1973*

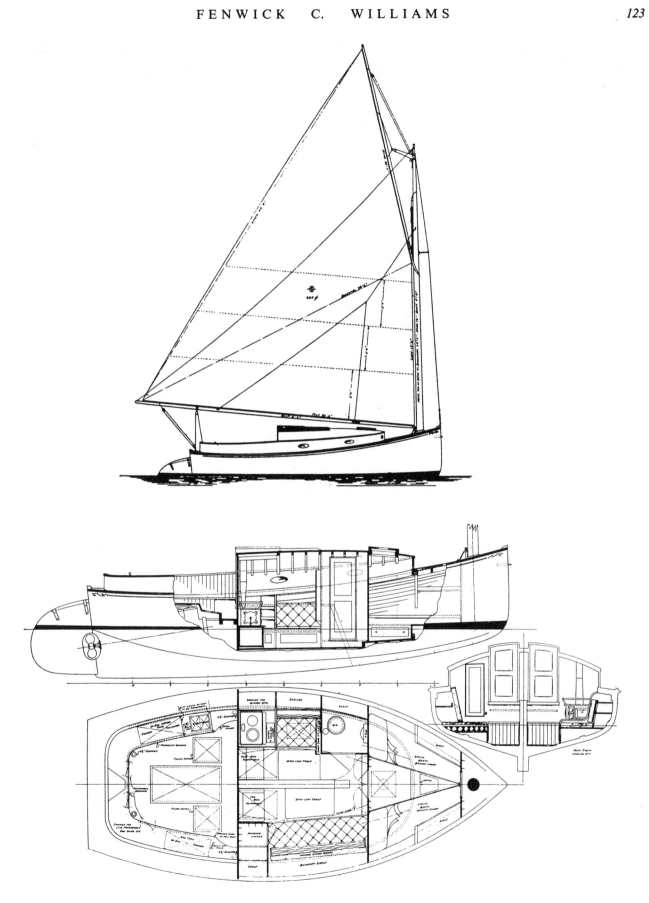

CHARLES W. WITTHOLZ

52

Prudence

Length on Deck: 25 feet 2 inches
Length on Waterline: 23 feet 10 inches
Beam: 10 feet 6 inches
Draft: 2 feet 7 inches
Sail Area: 450 square feet
Designer: Charles W. Wittholz

An alumnus of the Philip L. Rhodes firm of naval architects, Charles W. Wittholz is a highly respected designer who has also had much experience with catboats.

His 25-foot *Prudence* is a Cape Cod type, but she has a yachtier stern with an underslung rudder, rather than

the outboard "barndoor" type of rudder. The rudder on *Prudence* is less prone to ventilating, but because it is somewhat hidden by the raking transom, you would have to be careful not to forget it was there when docking and maneuvering in close places.

Prudence has a less symmetrical hull with a finer

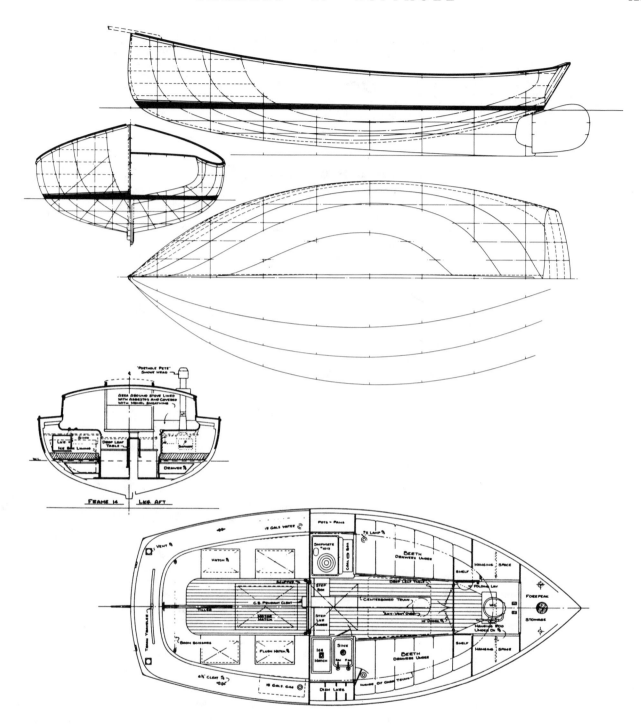

entry than the Williams-designed 21-footer (design No. 50). She should be able to cut through head seas well, but might be a slight bit wetter. Howard Chapelle wrote that some builders claim the hollow entrance with no shoulder increases weatherliness, but the feature might also increase weather helm when the stern is very full. An obvious advantage *Prudence* has over the 21-footer is that her larger size allows a larger galley with a more accessible icebox and an enclosed head.

In addition to the cat rig, the designer offers an alternate Noank sloop rig. The sloop rig affords a quick, easy means of shortening sail and relieves weather helm. The cat rig, however, is simpler and gets its area up higher in light airs. The short bowsprit with the cat rig provides a good angle for the forestay and a place to stow (I won't say *cat*) the anchor.

Plans from The Catboat Book, *edited by John M. Leavens, International Marine, 1973*

53

Departure

Length on Deck: 35 feet
Length on Waterline: 27 feet 10 inches
Beam: 10 feet 5 inches
Draft: 4 feet 3 inches
Displacement: 15,300 pounds
Sail Area: 600 square feet
Designer: Charles W. Wittholz

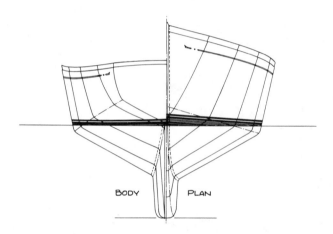

BODY   PLAN

This 35-foot ketch by Charles Wittholz is a hard-chine, vee-bottomed boat, shaped for ease of construction, whether she be built of wood or steel. She is another boat of many in this book that a skilled amateur can build at home. It is not easy to make a hard-chine hull beautiful, but Wittholz has pulled it off remarkably well. *Departure*'s looks are enhanced by a pleasing sheerline, nicely raked ends, a well-spooned bow, a rounded upper transom, and a gracefully shaped outboard rudder.

The rudder looks a bit small, but the boat can be made to balance well, and the cutaway forefoot helps give her maneuverability. There is ample flare forward for dryness and plenty of waterline length for good reaching performance. Her moderately shoal draft is not conducive to outstanding windward performance, but it allows her to enter shallow harbors without the hassle and complications of a centerboard.

The layout below is well proven. Although another version of this boat has quarter berths, which ease the motion for the offwatch at sea, quarter berths can get wet from spray blowing down the companionway, and there are good arguments for sleeping amidships. There is no chart table, but the top of the icebox could be used for this purpose, and the box's side door might be used when charts are on top.

A possible worthwhile alteration to the rig would be the addition of a short bowsprit. This would provide greater sail power and allow catting the anchor. It would also allow a more efficient jib if you wanted one that was self-tending.

Departure is a boat you would be proud to own, and you'd be twice as proud if you built her yourself.

Plans from The Proper Yacht, *Second Edition, by Arthur Beiser, International Marine, 1978*

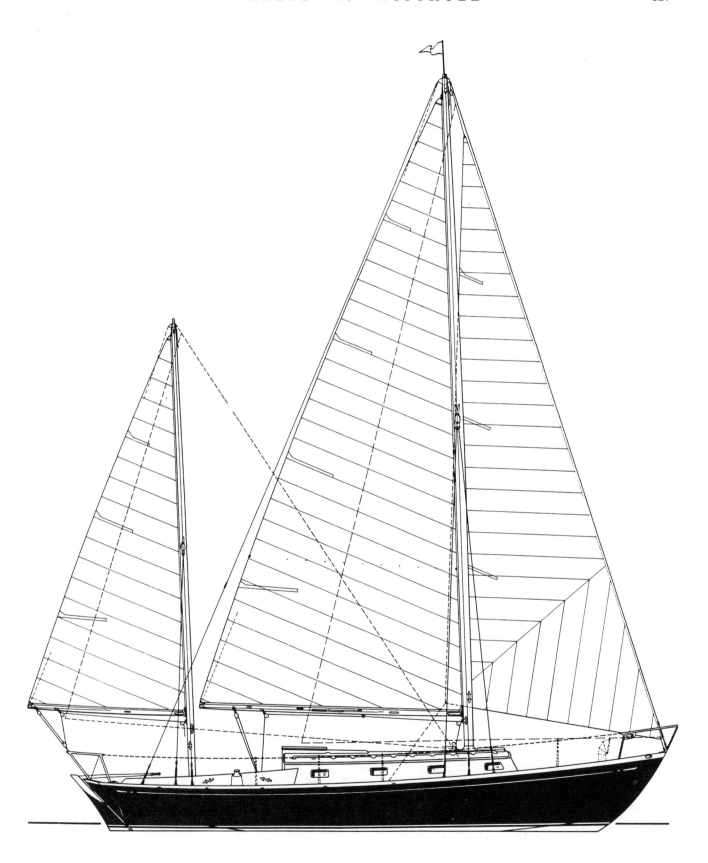

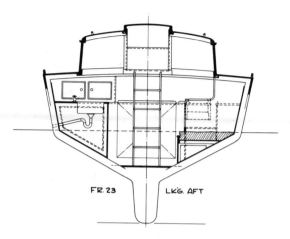

FR. 23   LK'G. AFT

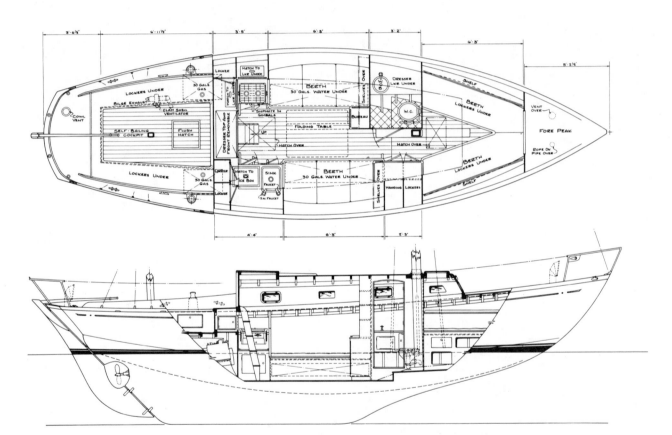

ADDRESSES OF THE DESIGNERS

John Atkin
P.O. Box 3005
Noroton, CT 06820

William Atkin
(from John Atkin)

Jay Benford
Jay R. Benford & Assoc., Inc.
758 Trenton Avenue
Severna Park, MD 21146

Philip C. Bolger
250 Washington Street
Gloucester, MA 01930

Edward Brewer
217 Edith Point Road
Anacortes, WA 98221

Samuel S. Crocker, Jr.
(from Sturgis Crocker
Crocker Boat Yard
P.O. Box 253, Ashland Avenue
Manchester, MA 01915)

William Garden
2071 Kendal Avenue
Victoria, B.C., Canada
W8P 1R7

Thomas C. Gillmer
1 Shipwright Harbor
Annapolis, MD 21402

Jay Hanna
Spear Street
Rockport, ME 04856

L. Francis Herreshoff
(from Muriel M. Vaughn
Herreshoff Castle
2 Crocker Park
Marblehead, MA 01945)

Al Mason
P.O. Box 5177
Virginia Beach, VA 23455

C. W. Paine
Yacht Design Inc.
Main Street
Tenants Harbor, ME 04860

Murray J. Peterson
(from William Peterson
Jones Cove
South Bristol, ME 04568)

Fenwick C. Williams
c/o William Peterson
Jones Cove
South Bristol, ME 04568

Charles W. Wittholz
100 Williamsburg Drive
Silver Spring, MD 20901